The Big Green Poetry Machine

Poetic Visions
Edited by Annabel Cook

First published in Great Britain in 2009 by:

Young Writers
Remus House
Coltsfoot Drive
Peterborough
PE2 9JX
Telephone: 01733 890066
Website: www.youngwriters.co.uk

All Rights Reserved
Book Design by Spencer Hart & Tim Christian
© Copyright Contributors 2008
SB ISBN 978-1-84924-055-0

Foreword

Young Writers' Big Green Poetry Machine is a showcase for our nation's most brilliant young poets to share their thoughts, hopes and fears for the planet they call home.

Young Writers was established in 1991 to nurture creativity in our children and young adults, to give them an interest in poetry and an outlet to express themselves. Seeing their work in print will encourage them to keep writing as they grow, and become our poets of tomorrow.

Selecting the poems has been challenging and immensely rewarding. The effort and imagination invested by these young writers makes their poems a pleasure to enjoy reading time and time again.

Contents

Shrinidhi Prakash (6) 1

Backwell CE Junior School, Backwell
Lauren Tavener (10) 1
Thomas Morley (10) 2
Liorah Barratt (10) 2
Kieran Dyer (9) 3
Charlotte Boddy (8) 3
Danika Cogan (11) 4
Ebony Love (10) 4
Tom Hewitt (10) 5
Verity Saville (10) 5
Ellie Parker (10) 6
Nancy Hull (9) 6
Adam Crawford (10) 7
Avisa Curtis (9) 7
Ellie Scott-Brown (9) 8
Hester Battin (9) 8
Sarah Llewellyn (9) 9
Zachary Nanji-Pritchard (9) 9
Izzi Hewitt & Milly Overton (8) 10
Alice Ellison (10) 10
Emma Miles (10) 11
Genevieve Sabherwal (10) 11
Michael James Proffitt (10) 12
Jessica Hartrey (10) 12
Maddie Black (10) 12
Reece Jordan Cogzell (10) 13
James Hatcher (10) 13
Josh Lewis (10) 13
Lydia Mahdjoubi (10) 14
Paige Brown (10) 14
Bethany Fowler (9) 14
Alex Andersson (11) 15
Freya Dix (10) 15
William Solari (11) 15
Tamsin Morris (10) 16
Bethany Watkins (10) 16
Jonathan Murray (9) 16
Ellie Redfern (9) 17
Eva Hughes (9) 17
Harriet Moore (10) 17
Thomas Ettle (11) 18
Alex Camm (9) 18
Aimee Irvine (11) 18
Emma Baber (10) 19
Michael Askew (10) 19
Natalia Barge (9) 19
Cameron Jupp (10) 20
Harrison Gould (10) 20
Molly Huckle (9) 20
Nathan Sharpe (10) 21
Dan Bewley (9) 21

Benson Community School, Hockley
Jade Elise Kaur Gill (7) 21
Chadwick Peart (8) 22
Adeeba Suleman (6) 22
Achli Bell, Ajay Mall, Zoe Wiseman,
Joshua Jackson, Shamaree (6)
& Fatou Ceesay (7) 23
Ange Nzeyimana (7) 23
Jamani McCooty (7) 24
Armaan Abid (7) 24
Corey Broughton (7) 24
Kian O'Keeffe (8) 25
Mohima Ali (8) 25
Faith Joy Woolley (7) 25
Demarné Valentino Bailey (7) 26
Kieron Taylor (6) 26
Adornie Irish (7) 26
Ameera Nasim (7) 27
Shemarley Bernard (7) 27
Jasmeena Kumari Badhan (7) 27
Fadumah Shire (6) 28
Rolonda Gouldbourne (6) 28
Sumeeya Afzal (7) 28
Dijonaé Kerr-Goodin (6) 29
Sophie Munganga (7) 29
Mariam Ahmed (7) 29
Priya Kaur Flora (8) 30
Taslima Ali (7) 30

Tyrelle Cohen (7) 30
Mya Brooks (7) 31
Brianna Martin (6) 31
Sameer Ghalib (7) 31
Harris Mahmood (6) 32
Adil Afiez (7) 32
Nadeem Zaman (6) 32
Hamza Azram (6) 33
Prabhjot Kaur (8) 33
Dylan Mahay (7) 33
Alfie Mellor Weeks (6) 34
Tatiana Tulloch (8) 34
Aaron Badhan (6) 34
Rowan By (7) 35

British Embassy Study Group, Turkey
Enis Tokcan (10) 35
Nazli Saatcioglu (8) 36
James Patrick Godfrey (7) 36
Zehra Alten (10) 37
Muntaka Ahmed (9) 37
Ariana Lanzer (10) 38
Zofia Wilczek (9) 38
Vivian Melder (11) 39
Ilse Alfonsi (10) 39
Alexandria Pacheco (Lexy) (8) 40
Mert Erden (10) 40
Giampaolo Servida (8) 41
St John Cooper (9) 41
Alpin Deda (8) 42
Samantha Noelle Atherton (7) 42
Peter Godfrey (8) 43
Aylin Laity (10) 43
Berke Nzliaka (8) 43
Bora Sayer (8) 44
Begum Gürel (8) 44
Manul Semtner (8) 44
Derya Simsek (7) 45
Nikki Wright (10) 45
Kemal Akman (7) 45
Zeynep Yilal (9) 46
Niklas Johnson (8) 46

Christ Church CE Primary School, Birkenhead
Lauren Simpson (10) 46
Ceri Sullivan (11) 47
Kelsie Day (10) 47
Kayleigh Bett (10) 48
Samantha Murray (10) 48
Matthew Wheeler (11) 49
Courtney Guy (10) 49
Kevin Day (10) 50
Charlie Shaw (10) 50
Michelle Olugbode (10) 51

Copeland Road Primary School, West Auckland
Mica Newcomb (10) 51
Milly Armstrong (10) 51
Luke Berry (10) 52
Ellie Douthwaite (10) 52

Flora Stevenson Primary School, Edinburgh
Holly McNab (6) 52
Rebecca Jack (7) 53
Maisie Evans (6) 53
Jack Bennie (7) 54
Maalavisha Sankar (7) 54
David Hale (8) 54
Keanna Mair (7) 55
Owen Readman (7) 55
Ryan Thomas (7) 55
Lisa Gray (7) 56
Max Fleming (7) 56
Kris Gaff (7) 56
Shaun McGrath (8) 57
India Lloyd (7) 57
Matthew Bagshaw (7) 57
Amelia Mapson (8) 58

Great Kingshill CE Combined School, High Wycombe
Matthew Price (8) 58
Olivia Blake (8) 59

Myles Stroud (8)	59
Harry Knightley (8)	60
Hasan Ishaq (8)	60
Alice Rudkin (8)	61
Maddy Bridges (8)	61
Claudia Cook (8)	62
Thomas Lundie-Sadd (8)	62
Jodie Neal (9)	63
Bismah Hussain (9)	63
Catriona Roberts (8)	64
Thomas Williams (9)	64
Charlotte Bellamy (8)	64
Kimberley Rickards (8)	65
Rachel Stewart (8)	65
Lily Hansford (8)	65
Fintan Jenkinson (8)	66
Amy Williams	66
Abigail Pinner (8)	66
Jessica Dixon (9)	67
Robert Smith (8)	67
Gabbie Fountain (8)	67
Alexa Tunnicliffe (8)	68
George Keeley (9)	68
James Dixon (9)	68
Yasmin Richardson (9)	69
Lily Hughes (8)	69
Luke Donnellan	69
Patrick Orford (8)	70
Max Grimmett (8)	70
Jasper Garofalo (8)	70
Eddie Colwill (9)	71
Eloise Godfrey (8)	71
Oliver Martins (8)	71
Ollie Dixon	72
Harry King (8)	72
Afsa Hussain (9)	72

Hartside Primary School, Crook

Ryan Easthaugh	73
Sophie Hauxwell	73
Melissa Jones	74
Niamh Blackett	74
Timothy Collyer	75
Caine Longstaff	75
Jasmine Moore	76

Michael Craggs	76
Rowan Hope	77
Ellie McGurk	77
Dylan Quinn	77
Bailey Colman	78
Jack Hodgson	78
Jak Crocher	78
Tom Sheppard	79

Latymer All Saints CE Primary School, Edmonton

Mathushan Krishnakumar	79
Rianna Marquis	80
Promise Emesi (8)	80
Dorcas Basia	81
Allysia Cunningham	81
Temi Adegbayibi	82
Seline Ansal	82
Godgift Emesi (10)	83

Lochdar School, Lochdar

Hugh Paterson (8)	83

Lowca Community School, Whitehaven

Denica Whinn (9)	84
Luke Johnston (10)	85
Jason Fleming (11)	86
Megan Foster (10)	86
Jake Martin (11)	87
Charlie Walker (10)	87
Leona Jolly (9)	88
Rebecca Iredale (9)	88
Marcus Maudlin (9)	89
Jessica Johnston (10)	89
James McNally (10)	90
Jordan Hetherington (9)	90

Manchester Muslim Preparatory School, Withington

Maliha Ahmed (8)	91
Umar Rashid (8)	91
Saarah Choudary (8)	92
Seif Mohammed (9)	92
Alani Anazim (8)	93
Faiz Mohammed (8)	93

Talha Khan (9) 94
Hamza Haq (8) 94
Aqsa Saied (9) 95
Amirah Mohammed (8) 95
Yusuf Mahmoud (8) 96
Subaat Rathur (8) 96
Faris Akhtar (8) 96

Pardes House Primary School, Finchley
Avi Garson (9) 97
Motti Stern (10) 97
Motty Sprung (9) 98
Modchele Kahan (10) 98
Pinchos Dunner (9) 99
Dovy Palmer (9) 99

Priory Primary School, Hull
Rosy Dias (10) 100
Chloe Corlass (10) 100
Georgia Green (10) 101
Thomas Gleadhill (10) 101
Declan Hall (10) 102
Bethany Soulsby (11) 102
Joshua Streets-Wray (10) 103
Charlotte Briggs (11) 103
Alex Jenkins (10) 104
Liam Old (10) 104
Laura Fee (10) 105
Matthew Robinson (11) 105
Halil Onay (10) 106
Leonie Wright (10) 106
Charlie Sommerville (10) 107
Jessica Mason (10) 107
Joshua Iles-Caville (11) 108
Jake Cooper (10) 108
Max Palmer (11) 109
Courtney Ferrie (10) 109
Shannon Brinkley (10) 110

Rector Drew School, Hawarden
Bethan Cooper (10) 110
Megan Elizabeth Rowlands,
Eithne Preece (10) & Lauren Jones (11) 111
Kate Newby (7) 111

Tom Williams (10) 112
Katie McLoughlin (8) 112
Jennifer Blythe (10) 113
Abi Shevlin (9) 113
Megan Rendle (10) 114
Madeleine Dibble (8) 114
Edward Williams (10) 115
Charlotte Naylor (10) 115
Jenny Hughes (8) 116
Tom Kennedy (8) 116
Adam Brooke-Jones (8) 117
Liam Collins (8) 117
Michael Warrenger (10) 118
Lucy Harrison (7) 118
Thomas Janney (10) 119
Zoe Watson (8) 119
Charlotte Anderton (9) 120
Hannah Baker (8) 120
Eleanor Crawford (8) 121
Michael Preston (10) 121
Harrison Hayes (8) 122
Louis Kennedy (10) 122
Jack Baker (11) 123
Polly Keeling (11) 123
Sam Dibble (10) 123
Deryn Wakefield (11) 124

Richmond Hill Primary School, Aspatria
Leonie Thompson (8) 124
Alix Long (8) 124
Jonathan Love (8) 125
Steven Crake (8) 125
Matthew Charlton (8) 125
Dylan McTear (8) 126
Callum Rogers (8) 126

Springfield Primary School, Tilehurst
Srihari Prasad Bhallamudi (10) 127

Tayyibah Girls' School, Stamford Hill
Anisa Kantharia 127
Suhaa Mahmood 128
Zaynab Almeriouh 129

Louisa Benatallah 129
Nasimah Galiara 130
Ayesha Chowdhury 130
Amina Atchoum 131
Iman Atchoum 131
Tahani Ali 132
Ilham Kemal 132
Mariam Patel 133
Hadjar Sebaa 133
Shakira Begum 134

The Poems

My Green Thumb

Green! Green! Green!
What a wonderful scene!

Do not cut that tree!
Hope you will agree!

Trees never demand fees,
For their delicious feasts!

Grow many a plant,
They really enchant.

Have a kitchen garden,
Being a 'green' captain.

Say 'no' to beach litter,
As animals feel bitter.

Make our Earth clean,
Let that be our dream!

Shrinidhi Prakash (6)

I Wish

I wish I could stop the wars today,
And would the Earth be a better place?
All the sadness all the time,
No more sad lives on the line.

I wish I could stop global warming,
The Earth's heating up, that's a warming,
Cancel junk mail, we don't need it,
Don't use emails, let's delete it.

I wish I could save rainforests,
That's what we need to do,
They all stand tall, they should not fall,
But that's what they seem to do.

Lauren Tavener (10)
Backwell CE Junior School, Backwell

Tips For Recycling

Walk, run, cycle,
Reduce, reuse, recycle.

The problem with litter,
Is when it's dumped, the air gets bitter.

Walk, run, cycle,
Reduce, reuse, recycle.

Smoke from the tower,
By the way, don't waste time in the shower.

Walk, run, cycle,
Reduce, reuse, recycle.

Don't cut down the trees,
They're home to the bees.

Walk, run, cycle,
Reduce, reuse, recycle.

Thomas Morley (10)
Backwell CE Junior School, Backwell

Look At The World

Look at the trees,
All burning down,
Why are we all
Polluting the air?

Look at the cars,
Everywhere a smokin'
Why are we all
Driving around?

Look at the animals,
Lost in smoke,
Why do they all
Have to suffer?

Liorah Barratt (10)
Backwell CE Junior School, Backwell

The Environmental Tree Poem

To save
The environment,
You need to
Reduce, reuse, recycle.
The world needs saving,
Use more buses, use more trains,
Before it starts to
Rain!
Walk
Or run,
Use the
Bike,
Don't
Use
Planes.

Kieran Dyer (9)
Backwell CE Junior School, Backwell

Save Our Planet

S olar panels,
A nimals need saving,
V ery little time to save our planet,
E ndangering Earth.

O ur Arctic ice is melting,
U nlimited energy from sun and wind,
R educe, reuse, recycle.

P olar bears and penguins need the ice,
L ower our carbon emissions,
A ntarctica is melting away,
N ature must survive,
E nvironmental pollution must stop,
T urn off lights, turn down the heat.

Charlotte Boddy (8)
Backwell CE Junior School, Backwell

Empty Rainforest

R ecycle, reduce and reuse,
A nimals are becoming extinct because of us,
I n the forest you will see what we are doing to the trees,
N ow look at the animals, what do you see? The guilty faces of you and me!
F ire and fumes we are breathing in but that's what the animals are living with,
O zone layer is getting old, please help it to revolve,
R easons why the oil in rivers make the fish die,
E veryone knows but no one stops, I don't know why and I'm beginning to cry,
S oon everything will be gone, the sea, the sky, but not a sound to be heard,
T o the flower, to the mountain, they're all the same and they're gone and you're to blame.

Danika Cogan (11)
Backwell CE Junior School, Backwell

Save The World

The ozone layer is breaking,
Way out in time and space,
So look after the planet,
And make the world a better place.

Because of global warming and
The melting of the ice caps,
Try and use less energy and turn off all the running taps,
The pollution from the aeroplanes,
And all that electricity from the mains,
Turn off all the lights,
And don't go on lots of flights,
Save the world!

Ebony Love (10)
Backwell CE Junior School, Backwell

An Empty World

S top that now!
A nimals are dying because of us,
V ery bad thing will happen,
E veryone can help,

T heir lives are in our hands,
H urry, or it'll be too late,
E verything will die.

A nimals and humans can be at peace,
N ever ever give up,
I f we stop now we will live,
M any are dying because we live,
A nimals are the light of the world,
L ong gone, an empty planet,
S adness will fill the world.

Tom Hewitt (10)
Backwell CE Junior School, Backwell

The World Needs You

Think of the creatures,
All the animals and plants,
Think of every time you
Go on an aeroplane,
Watch telly,
Even flick on a light,
The world is slowly dying.

But you can help,
Reduce,
Reuse,
Recycle,
The world needs your help,
And together the world,
Will be a better place.

Verity Saville (10)
Backwell CE Junior School, Backwell

Start Before It's Too Late

We can reduce rubbish, pollution and all that,
Sometimes it's just a button or easier than that,
Don't leave things on standby,
Just turn them off,
Walk short journeys, you will save,
A lot!
If you don't recycle, you can always reuse,
Things like cardboard would be great for a pretend car!

So please help the world,
You can make a difference,
But start now
Before it's too late.

Ellie Parker (10)
Backwell CE Junior School, Backwell

A Poem Of The Future

E nvironment, the first who stands tall and strong,
N aughty rubbish that we try not to use,
V entilate the world with the 3 Rs,
I nside our homes we have just arrived,
   because we went to recycle our stuff,
R educe, reuse and recycle, the three words we need in our world,
O h no, too much rubbish destroying nature,
N o more rubbish being chucked in the bins,
M ention the 3 Rs to all your friends,
E nd pollution by not using cars,
N ever forget this information,
T ell everyone to start recycling.

Nancy Hull (9)
Backwell CE Junior School, Backwell

Save The Environment

We must protect the environment,
It is in serious threat,
From the loss of trees
And the pollution from cars,
We must cut down on this,
Please help us save the environment,
We all have to do our bit,
To help stop global warming,
And to recycle,
If we don't stop killing trees,
We will kill ourselves,
So we have no choice but to save the environment.

Adam Crawford (10)
Backwell CE Junior School, Backwell

Environment

E nvironment's the best,
N o wasting allowed, just reuse, reduce, recycle,
V ary your walk,
I n your waste, make sure it can be,
R educed, reused, recycled,
O n the way to school, on your bike,
N o cars are allowed, take the bus to school,
M ake the world a better place, the three Rs,
E co-friendly kids could save the world, think,
N o more waste please,
T ell people about the world.

Avisa Curtis (9)
Backwell CE Junior School, Backwell

Help!

E at food with recyclable packaging,
N ever throw away things you can recycle,
V ending machines don't use, cos they use too much electricity,
I t's up to you to save the world,
R emember to cycle, not use the car,
O h please help otherwise we'll be dead,
N ever say no to recycling,
M ake a difference so we can live,
E nvironment is bad at the moment,
N ever kill animals so they can have a life,
T ake part for the sake of the world!

Ellie Scott-Brown (9)
Backwell CE Junior School, Backwell

Environment

E ven though some people don't care,
N ew things shouldn't be everywhere,
V ery bent things you can repair,
I hope that most of you do really care,
R epairing really is not hard,
O pen your tool box that's in the yard,
N ewspaper recycles, so does card
M ake your bent things look brand new,
E ven if it is your loo,
N ever, ever, ever give up,
T hese kind of things really aren't hard.

Hester Battin (9)
Backwell CE Junior School, Backwell

Stop Litter

S top all the litter,
T ry and get environment-friendly things,
O r the world could get destroyed,
P lease stop littering.

L itter makes people ill,
I t will save the environment if you try hard,
T hings will all get better,
T he world needs to stop littering,
E veryone can help,
R educe, reuse and recycle, it really will help!

Sarah Llewellyn (9)
Backwell CE Junior School, Backwell

Environmental Rap

Reduce, reuse, recycle, you just need to think,
Reduce, reuse, recycle, there is a simple link,
So when you turn on the tap,
You'll be chanting this rap!
With the endangered species . . .
Thinking about the black bear,
It has its own lair,
Give it a care!
So give it a try,
Before we all die!

Zachary Nanji-Pritchard (9)
Backwell CE Junior School, Backwell

Heal The World

When people cut down trees,
It makes us feel bad,
All the wonderful animals,
It's really sad,
Please help the world, make it a better place,
It won't feel such a big disgrace,
Please help the world, make it a better place,
It won't feel such a big disgrace,
All the precious creatures will disappear,
Without your help!

Izzi Hewitt & Milly Overton (8)
Backwell CE Junior School, Backwell

Rainforest

R euse, reduce, recycle,
A nd make sure you use it,
I n our world we are finding it hard,
N obody is doing anything about it,
F orests have feelings too,
O ur planet needs to be saved,
R educe people cutting down trees,
E verlasting rainforests would be cool,
S o stop destroying animals' habitats,
T hink of what would happen if there were no rainforests.

Alice Ellison (10)
Backwell CE Junior School, Backwell

The Environment

Our environment is getting even worse
And it's all up to you,
So listen to me now and
There's something you can do!
Turn the lights off when you're done,
Use a solar panel on your house,
It attracts the sun,
Reduce, reuse, recycle,
It will help your world,
Walk a lot more, that includes boys and girls.

Emma Miles (10)
Backwell CE Junior School, Backwell

My Planet

The world is in trouble with all the pollution,
So we've got to come up with a solution.

Look all around at all the trees,
We would not have them without bumblebees.

Turn off the heating and put on a jumper,
Don't put your rubbish in the dumper.

So reduce, reuse and recycle,
Do it now!

Genevieve Sabherwal (10)
Backwell CE Junior School, Backwell

Littering

L itter, it will never do, no, no, no,
I t's using up the Earth's green land,
T errified I am,
T errible we are, terrible, terrible, terrible,
E verything we can do, we need to do it now,
R ed-hot the Earth will be, so stop it now,
I ngenious scientists should have thought about it now,
N ever again will it happen if we solve it this time,
G reen we need to be, green, green, green.

Michael James Proffitt (10)
Backwell CE Junior School, Backwell

Our World

P edal to work instead of driving,
O ur cars should not be used,
L itter destroys the Earth, so stop,
L iving like this is so bad,
U nfortunately animals are dying every day,
T ighten your coats and start walking,
I n case in 6.5 million years the Earth will be gone,
O ff we go to recycle, reduce and reuse,
N ow if that happens, it will be a better place.

Jessica Hartrey (10)
Backwell CE Junior School, Backwell

There Once Was A Man Called Bill

There once was a man called Bill,
Who wanted to empty landfill,
He saved the world,
With his hair that was curled
And he continues to do it still.

Maddie Black (10)
Backwell CE Junior School, Backwell

Pollution

Stop all the pollution,
To save our planet,
Or it will get destroyed,
So please stop pollution,
Please stop all pollution,
Or there will be consequences,
Like the planet being destroyed,
You wouldn't want that,
So stop pollution.

Reece Jordan Cogzell (10)
Backwell CE Junior School, Backwell

My Rap

Being green isn't about people rabbiting on,
It's about working hard until the pollution is gone,
So don't be a lazy man who drives everywhere,
Be a man who pays a bus fare.

You've also gotta think about your energy,
So don't just put it on standby when you switch off the TV!
It's not just the telly you shouldn't leave on standby,
There are so many things to turn off, I could say em till I die.

James Hatcher (10)
Backwell CE Junior School, Backwell

Reduce, Reuse, Recycle Poem

Reduce, reuse, recycle - cycle your way to school,
Reduce, reuse, recycle - reduce the amount you waste,
Reduce, reuse, recycle - reuse things you're done with,
Reduce, reuse, recycle - recycle things like metal,
Reduce, reuse, recycle - now you know what to do.

Josh Lewis (10)
Backwell CE Junior School, Backwell

Save The Animals

S nakes and elephants all wild and free,
A nd here come the humans told to leave them be,
V andalised trees calling for help,
E ach animal known by its dying yelp.

T o save them we need to take drastic action,
H *elp them, help them!* No time for reaction,
E ventually they will be cured,
M aybe this message will be heard.

Lydia Mahdjoubi (10)
Backwell CE Junior School, Backwell

Save The Animals

Lots of creatures in our world,
And each one is great,
All of them in your hands,
You help decide their fate.

Black, white, fat or thin,
Frightened, fierce or kind,
Each animal should be loved,
Whether it can see or is blind.

Paige Brown (10)
Backwell CE Junior School, Backwell

Help Our World!

Come on, help make the world a better place,
Wipe greenhouse gases off the world's face,
Turn off every light not needed in sight,
Because this world's not going down without a big fight,
Everyone can take part,
Now this poem's finished, it's time to start.

Bethany Fowler (9)
Backwell CE Junior School, Backwell

Friends Of Mine

A ll of us should help animals,
N one of us should use too much wood,
I nstead use local leaves not trees,
M ake a difference and help them,
A ll animals deserve a say,
L ions, lemurs, penguins, parrots and foxes too,
S peak out for them as they are friends of yours, and friends of mine too.

Alex Andersson (11)
Backwell CE Junior School, Backwell

How To Get A Green World

Be kind to animals, do not kill,
Otherwise beautiful animals will become extinct,
Do not litter, it causes pollution,
The extraordinary world will die,
Pollution causes global warming,
We want this world to be green and healthy,
Use more pots to put food in,
Otherwise all of your rubbish will go to landfill sites.

Freya Dix (10)
Backwell CE Junior School, Backwell

Litter

L itter should be thrown away,
I f you chuck it on the floor,
T he world will be littered with litter,
T ons of litter is thrown away,
E ven when you know what will happen to Earth,
R ecycle your litter because that will make your world
a much better place.

William Solari (11)
Backwell CE Junior School, Backwell

Recycle

R educe, reuse, recycle,
E ncourage people to turn off lights,
C ut car journeys by giving your neighbour a lift to school,
Y ou should try and walk,
C ycle to school, don't drive,
L earn more,
E at less meat.

Tamsin Morris (10)
Backwell CE Junior School, Backwell

Stop

The world is getting worse day by day,
Stop buying things, you cannot recycle or just don't throw it away,
We're having the wrong weather at the wrong time,
I'm telling you to stop, I mean I'm right,
I wish you could just stop global warming,
Landfill sites and pollution,
Just stop!

Bethany Watkins (10)
Backwell CE Junior School, Backwell

Remember

Remember to be careful,
Remember to be good,
Remember, remember,
Remember the save the environment,
Remember the three Rs,
Reduce, reuse, recycle,
It's all up to you to remember!

Jonathan Murray (9)
Backwell CE Junior School, Backwell

What's Happening?

What is happening to our world?
I really want to know,
Is the snow and ice melting,
Or turning into snow?
Is everyone in town dropping litter on the ground,
So all the animals get ill?
Because if they are, it's gotta be bad!

Ellie Redfern (9)
Backwell CE Junior School, Backwell

No, No, No!

I was driving in my car one day,
But then someone said, 'No, no, no!'
Then I was chopping down a tree and
They said, 'No, no, no!'
Then I turned on a light and
Left it on and they said,
'No, no, no!'

Eva Hughes (9)
Backwell CE Junior School, Backwell

Save Our World!

The world needs our help,
And that help is growing your own food,
No chopping down trees,
No going out of a room
Without turning off the light,
The world needs to be saved,
Now!

Harriet Moore (10)
Backwell CE Junior School, Backwell

Help!

Help the world by doing this,
Don't drop litter, get rid of the tips.

Stop pollution taking hold,
Don't let global warming mould the way we live as a whole.

Animals are dying now, save them by not cutting down the forests,
And the woods, the trees would cut you down if they could.

Thomas Ettle (11)
Backwell CE Junior School, Backwell

The Environment

The environment needs help,
So come on and give a yelp,
We need a solution,
For all this pollution,
So when it's night,
Turn off that light.

Alex Camm (9)
Backwell CE Junior School, Backwell

Stop, Look And Think

Stop and look around you,
Just look at all the litter,
Look at it,
Think about it hard,
Maybe you could help
By reusing, reducing and recycling.

Aimee Irvine (11)
Backwell CE Junior School, Backwell

Reduce!

R educe, reuse, recycle,
E at less meat,
D on't leave any items on standby,
U se clothes lines instead of your dryer,
C ut car journeys by giving your friends lifts to places,
E ncourage people to turn off lights.

Emma Baber (10)
Backwell CE Junior School, Backwell

Litter

L itter is really bad,
I t is killing some animals,
T he green land is vanishing,
T errible things will happen,
E ventually there will be no room for landfill sites,
R emember what you have just read.

Michael Askew (10)
Backwell CE Junior School, Backwell

The Environment

The world is sad, it wasn't before,
Don't use planes and all the rest,
Use bikes, buses and trains
And the world will be happy again,
Some people care, some people don't,
But the good thing is that we will all help.

Natalia Barge (9)
Backwell CE Junior School, Backwell

Owls

Owls, owls everywhere,
They hoot here, they hoot there,
But please, oh please, use your head,
Owls hoot but if you pollute,
They'll be dead.

Cameron Jupp (10)
Backwell CE Junior School, Backwell

Recycle

The daisies are dying and so is the wood,
So start recycling before they're gone for good,
So use less electric or else I'll go hectic,
Reduce, reuse, recycle.

Harrison Gould (10)
Backwell CE Junior School, Backwell

A Whale Is A Whale

A dog is a dog,
A cat is a cat,
But a whale is not a whale,
Because you're killing them all.

Molly Huckle (9)
Backwell CE Junior School, Backwell

The Environment

Stop the cars from polluting the air,
Stop people chucking rubbish in the sea,
And the people that throw the cans
In the bin are wrong, wrong, wrong.

Nathan Sharpe (10)
Backwell CE Junior School, Backwell

Trees

Big green tree,
Swaying in the breeze,
Don't chop it down,
It's a big green tree!

Dan Bewley (9)
Backwell CE Junior School, Backwell

I Like Clean Air

I like the clean air,
Please keep the street clean,
I like the green to be seen,
Pick up the litter and put it in the bin,
So our bins,
Can be filled to the brims.

Don't chop down trees please,
I don't know what happens to the clean air,
It might be going into my hair,
I need to be sweeping,
Otherwise you'll be weeping.

The water will be leaking,
Then you will be shrieking.

Jade Elise Kaur Gill (7)
Benson Community School, Hockley

Clean Street

That's right children clean the street,
I don't want to see litter under my feet,
Please do not make a mess,
You make me very sad.

Come on children, stamp your feet,
Please don't chop the trees
Because we won't breathe.

Come on children,
Put your litter in the bin,
Because leaving rubbish would be a sin!

Chadwick Peart (8)
Benson Community School, Hockley

Untitled

Stop wasting water,
Always turn off the lights,
Very few people save energy,
Everybody is not turning off taps.

Everyone can save energy,
Never lose energy so turn off the TV.
Energy is precious,
Recycle your waste,
Go on and turn off the TV.

You have to turn off lights at night!

Adeeba Suleman (6)
Benson Community School, Hockley

Better Planet

I dropped litter and the binman became bitter.

If you don't pick up your litter,
You will get sprayed with glitter.

Keep your environment clean otherwise the
Animals will be mean.

So be good and bin it,
Keep your world and planet
As clean as it can be.

Achli Bell, Ajay Mall, Zoe Wiseman, Joshua Jackson, Shamaree (6) & Fatou Ceesay (7)
Benson Community School, Hockley

Untitled

Give me litter, give me dinner,
I want gum,
I want packets,
Give me it all and I'll be done,
Stop that throwing,
Stop that littering,
You know what to do,
Just put it in my tummy, mmmm,
Stop that madness, you're giving me a headache!

Ange Nzeyimana (7)
Benson Community School, Hockley

War

People dying,
People fighting,
No more war,
People dying,
Blood dripping,
People invading,
The world is sure,
I drop on my knees before I die,
Stop all this because I will cry.

Jamani McCooty (7)
Benson Community School, Hockley

Untitled

No more rubbish,
Come on children, let's clean my street,
Then I'll give you a treat,
Come on children, let's sweep around,
Then we'll have a fun night out,
And have a dance around,
Come on children, stamp your feet,
And pick up your rubbish,
Before the dustmen chop off your feet.

Armaan Abid (7)
Benson Community School, Hockley

Recycle

Let's recycle, let's clean up,
Pick up litter, recycle glass,
Put them in the bottle banks,
Let's reuse glass and paper,
Save it all and use it later.

Corey Broughton (7)
Benson Community School, Hockley

Untitled

Stop, stop, stop throwing litter,
I am shining, I want litter,
In my tum, I want gum in my tum,
I want crisp packets
And ice cream wrappers,
And all the other stuff,
I want to be dirty,
I am starving, I want food,
Make the world a better place.

Kian O'Keeffe (8)
Benson Community School, Hockley

Litter, Litter

Stop, stop, stop,
Don't throw litter,
Don't throw gum,
Put it in my tum.

Litter, litter,
On the floor,
Pick some more,
And clean some more.

Mohima Ali (8)
Benson Community School, Hockley

Untitled

I hate the dirt so please recycle the bottles and plastic,
Children come on, clean the street,
Otherwise the rats will come and invade the street,
Hurry up children, the rats are coming,
Quickly, clean the streets and let's get running.

Faith Joy Woolley (7)
Benson Community School, Hockley

Tidy Streets

Come on children, stamp your feet,
Pick up the rubbish and have a clean street.

Come on children, keep the streets clean,
Do not make rubbish take away the gleam.

Come on children, have a clean street,
Don't just stay around,
Get up on your feet and start cleaning the street.

Demarné Valentino Bailey (7)
Benson Community School, Hockley

Recycle And Reuse

Recycling helps the world be a clean environment
And helps you to be keen,
So nobody gets hurt by glass, or if there was a broken trumpet,
There would be some brass,
You can kill some animals, so come and recycle with Kieron.

Kieron is a number one recycler,
He is great at recycling everything!

Kieron Taylor (6)
Benson Community School, Hockley

Smoking

S top making smoke,
M ake the world a better place,
O nly take it out of your mouth,
K iller cigarettes can kill you,
I llnesses will make you vomit,
N ice places get smoke all over the place,
G etting diseases is spreading all over everyone.

Adornie Irish (6)
Benson Community School, Hockley

Smoking

S ome people smoke,
M ake sure you don't smoke,
O h no! Some people smoke,
K illers!
I don't smoke,
N ot putting cigarettes on the floor,
G ive people money for charity.

Ameera Nasim (7)
Benson Community School, Hockley

Turn Off

Turn off the heater,
Turn off the light,
Turn off the laptop,
Turn off the TV,
Turn off the Hoover,
Turn off the lamp,
Save electric, save the world.

Shemarley Bernard (7)
Benson Community School, Hockley

Untitled

Please don't chop down trees,
Don't chop down trees,
We need them to breathe,
Don't chop down trees,
Because they have leaves,
Please keep the street clean,
Because I like the green.

Jasmeena Kumari Badhan (7)
Benson Community School, Hockley

Smoking

S top smoking,
M ake sure you don't smoke,
O h no! I can see people smoking,
K illers!
I t can kill people,
N ever smoke in your whole life,
G ive up smoking.

Fadumah Shire (6)
Benson Community School, Hockley

Smoking

S ome people are smoking,
M y auntie and I wish that my auntie wouldn't smoke,
O h no, some people are smoking and that is not good,
K illing yourself,
I don't smoke, give up smoking,
N ever smoke,
G ive up smoking.

Rolonda Gouldbourne (6)
Benson Community School, Hockley

Smoking

S top smoking because the disease is coming,
M y pollution is disgusting because it's horrible,
O h no, the cough is rude and dirty germs,
K iller germs!
I n smoking, they will have bad breath or be sick,
N ever smoke, it's bad for the environment,
G ive up cigarettes!

Sumeeya Afzal (7)
Benson Community School, Hockley

My Rhyme Of Recycling

Paper, paper, cans and bottles,
Recycle, recycle shoes, clothes and toys.

See you later, see you later,
Recycle, recycle pictures, fixtures and mixtures,
Dijonaé says recycle your rubbish,
In such a way, it helps the environment every day.

Dijonaé Kerr-Goodin (6)
Benson Community School, Hockley

Litter

L ots of litter on the floor,
I t is very smelly,
T he litter is dirty,
T ake your rubbish home,
E veryone drops litter,
R ubbish has to go in the bin.

Sophie Munganga (7)
Benson Community School, Hockley

The Trees

Please don't chop the trees,
They help us to breathe,
Birds have their homes in trees,
If you chop the trees,
We won't have fruit or any air,
The birds will die!

Mariam Ahmed (7)
Benson Community School, Hockley

Save The Trees

Don't chop down the trees please,
Or we won't be able to breathe,
Don't chop down the trees please,
Or we will die without trees,
Don't chop down the trees please,
Or the animals will freeze.

Priya Kaur Flora (8)
Benson Community School, Hockley

Recycle

Come and read my poem,
It is about recycling,
I like to recycle paper, toys, glass and cans,
Clitter-clatter, clatter-clitter,
Pick up the litter,
Recycle is what we like to do.

Taslima Ali (7)
Benson Community School, Hockley

No Cutting Trees Please!

Please no cutting the trees,
Please we need them to grow fruits
And we need to breathe oxygen,
And the animals need to eat some leaves,
And the birds need to live in the trees,
So please don't cut down the trees.

Tyrelle Cohen (7)
Benson Community School, Hockley

Come On Children

Come on children, I don't want your rubbish,
Come on children, pick it up,
Come on children, clean the mess,
Come on children, save the planet,
Recycle your packets, recycle your bottles,
Recycle your paper.

Mya Brooks (7)
Benson Community School, Hockley

Litter

L itter should be in the bin,
I can pick up litter off the floor,
T ake some litter, lots off the floor,
T ry to pick up lots of litter,
E verybody pick up lots of litter,
R ecycle litter.

Brianna Martin (6)
Benson Community School, Hockley

Garbage

Today is the day of Environment Day,
I get rid of rubbish,
Throw away day, get rid of it today,
Make room to play, so I recycle away,
Toys, games, jars and Milky Bar wrappers,
Today is the day, throw away day.

Sameer Ghalib (7)
Benson Community School, Hockley

Litter

L itter is thrown in the bin,
I t is right to pick up litter,
T ime to pick up litter,
T ry to pick up litter,
E njoy picking up litter,
R ight to pick up litter all the time.

Harris Mahmood (6)
Benson Community School, Hockley

Don't Chop Down Trees

Please don't chop down trees,
Please don't chop down trees,
We need them to breathe,
Please don't chop down trees,
Please don't chop down trees,
Birds will die and I will cry.

Adil Afiez (7)
Benson Community School, Hockley

Jamie Jump

Jamie Jump is his name,
He loves the game of recycling rubbish,
Rubbish, throw it away, get rid of it for another day,
Jamie Jump recycles rubbish,
Cans, fans and pans,
Jump Jamie with joy, you make the environment clean and tidy.

Nadeem Zaman (6)
Benson Community School, Hockley

Litter

L itter looks messy,
I t blows around the street,
T ake your rubbish home,
T he litter should be binned,
E veryone has to take care of the planet,
R ecycle your litter.

Hamza Azram (6)
Benson Community School, Hockley

Recycle

Recycle bottles,
Recycle cardboard,
Make new newspapers,
Don't throw cans in the rivers,
The world will be clean,
So come on people, pick it up.

Prabhjot Kaur (8)
Benson Community School, Hockley

Recycling

Recycling glass and paper,
Helps to save our planet,
Recycling cans and cartons,
Helps to save our country,
Recycling boxes and paper,
Helps to save our world.

Dylan Mahay (7)
Benson Community School, Hockley

Recycle And Reduce

We need to stop dropping litter
Or our environment will be bitter.

So your papers, cans and bottles
Must be stored in our coloured plastic tubs.

Alfie Mellor Weeks (6)
Benson Community School, Hockley

Litter On The Street

Come on children,
I do not want any litter on the street.

Come on children,
Put the litter in the bin because leaving rubbish would be a sin!

Tatiana Tulloch (8)
Benson Community School, Hockley

Keeping Our Environment Clean

If you always litter, it can be bad for us and animals,
So it is important not to litter to keep our environment clean,
As a country, we should come together and keep
Our environment a healthy one.

Aaron Badhan (6)
Benson Community School, Hockley

Litter

Put a tin in a bin,
Pick up gum and then you won't be doing a sin,
Make the world a better place,
And create a happy space.

Rowan By (7)
Benson Community School, Hockley

The Greatest War

The blind eyes of human beings,
Cannot seek the wildest reaper,
For it is us,
Not tigers, lions or panthers,
But us,
You, me and us are the terror of creation,
The centre of this terrible event,
Is not just factories, log-cutters or poachers,
But all of us.

This war is greater than the World Wars,
The war of grey and green,
Humans conduct this swarming dark cloud,
Yet animals other than us, try to prevail,
The grey will win,
Unless we lessen it,
Which is a complex task for wicked humanity,
But can you help?
This is a world that is dying,
Is there still hope?

Enis Tokcan (10)
British Embassy Study Group, Turkey

Making The World A Healthier Place

When people are poor,
They easily get sick,
They go door by door,
To find food to pick.

Poor people lack everything,
They need a little help,
Let them keep hopes alive,
So their dreams come true.

Poverty is the worst sickness,
In the world of all,
We need to get rid of it,
For a better future for us.

Join me in this effort,
Don't leave yourself behind,
It is time to act now,
Or it will be late forever.

Nazli Saatcioglu (8)
British Embassy Study Group, Turkey

Argh! The Whales Are Dying!

Blue whales are giants,
Sharks are mostly scared,
Blue whales are very strong,
Blue whales' voices can beat a gong,
But why, oh why are the waters evaporating?
And the cars are making smoke and the blue whales
Breathe air and we're harpooning them.
It's happening in the Atlantic Ocean so we have to . . .
Stop harpooning!
Because of the name, you know it's blue and it's also white,
Blue whales eat shrimp and we're eating more,
Blue, blue, blue, blue, blue whales.

James Patrick Godfrey (7)
British Embassy Study Group, Turkey

Treating This World

How would you save the planet?
I would like to know,
I would stop littering in this world.

Why are you doing this?
Do you have a reason?

I do.
We became cruel, mean and horrible,
Killing our environment,
Causing dying to our animals,
Factories causing pollution,
And never caring about global warming,
Paying with really dirty money,
We should take this seriously and change
The ways we are treating our planet,
We should do better not being mean,
Try to be kind please.

Zehra Alten (10)
British Embassy Study Group, Turkey

Recycle!

Don't use too much oil,
Don't throw scraps or paper on soil,
Recycle! Recycle!
Don't burn too much gas,
Leave things alone and leave what it has,
Recycle! Recycle!
Don't leave things lying on the ground,
See litter and garbage will be found,
Recycle! Recycle!
Put things into green, red and blue bins,
Those will help you and many other things,
Recycle! Recycle!

Muntaka Ahmed (9)
British Embassy Study Group, Turkey

Go Green

The Earth is getting hotter
Day by day,
The ice caps are melting,
And the smoke
From factories is not helping,
And one day you'll regret not
Helping the world be better
Than it is today. So
Don't cut down trees, they give us air,
Stop polluting because the waste gets everywhere,
Don't poison the sea with factory goo,
And the animals are affected by this too,
So save the Earth, oh please do,
It's the only one we will ever have.
So go green,
Oh please do!

Ariana Lanzer (10)
British Embassy Study Group, Turkey

Rainforests

What is a rainforest?
I bet you'd like to know,
It's a place where animals live,
And many plants grow.

Butterflies float on a flower,
Every day, hour by hour,
Where can you find a toucan?
In the rainforest, of course you can!

There are millions of species,
Of animals, plants and trees,
But they are all disappearing,
They need your help, please!

Zofia Wilczek (9)
British Embassy Study Group, Turkey

Pollution In The World

These are facts about what is happening,
To the world . . .

Icebergs heating up
And polar bears with it.

Factories spreading smoke
And the blue sky with it.

Animals made into coats,
Trees getting cut up,
Floods growing wild,
Seas turning into oil,
Pollution isn't good at all!

Does the world need to be tortured?
. . . And us with it?

Vivian Melder (11)
British Embassy Study Group, Turkey

Global Warming

Cutting down trees,
The world getting polluted,
Bad floods eating land,
Will we ever save this world?

Wasting paper,
Throwing rubbish in the rivers,
Factories polluting things,
Will we ever save this world?

We're all in this together,
We know we can make things better,
It's today or never,
Let's save this world forever!

Ilse Alfonsi (10)
British Embassy Study Group, Turkey

All Around The World

Dogs on the street
Is not really neat,
The Big Green Poetry Machine,
Tyres on the floor make me bored,
The Big Green Poetry Machine,
Rubbish on the sand,
Doesn't make a lot of land,
The Big Green Poetry Machine,
Polar bears and penguins live on ice,
Ice is melting into dice,
The Big Green Poetry Machine.

Alexandria Pacheco (Lexy) (8)
British Embassy Study Group, Turkey

Last Life

Hey world! Don't cut the trees,
Oxygen is fading, such a waste of life,
Trash is increasing, pollution is increasing,
Thus we are decreasing,
All hope's not lost,
We can change this world to a
Slaughter-free, breathable place,
Imagine less factories, no endangered animals,
We can make this dump into an alien site,
So far we are carnivorous, not a crop to eat,
We can change this world, join the light.

Mert Erden (10)
British Embassy Study Group, Turkey

A World Without War

I would like to live in a world without wars,
Without people dying every day,
Without houses and trees being destroyed,
Is it possible?
I hope and I think so,
But how?
I'm only a child but I think
That adults need to play more,
And to read more fairy tales,
Because they have to nourish their minds,
With good thoughts.

Giampaolo Servida (8)
British Embassy Study Group, Turkey

Environmental Tale

E nd for all,
N one left,
V ery hot,
I ce melting,
R ubbish mountains,
O ur planet is dying,
N ets are catching all the fish,
M other Nature is not happy,
E lephants will soon be forgotten,
N o more bees,
T here is no hope unless we change.

St John Cooper (9)
British Embassy Study Group, Turkey

Untitled

There I was drinking water peacefully,
Water comes from clouds, water is healthy,
It's good for people,
People need water or else people will die,
Without water no one will live,
We need water, water is important,
Tell your friends to stop wasting water,
Everyone in the world needs water,
Any kind of water, people sell water to keep people alive,
We need to celebrate the people who treat our water as precious.

Alpin Deda (8)
British Embassy Study Group, Turkey

Florida Panther

One beautiful night in the forest,
There was a lovely sound,
Until the Florida panther,
A black and orange, very pretty, clever animal,
Roared as loud as she could,
Because there were men trying to take their habitat
And were cutting down the beautiful green trees,
When the panther scared the men to stop taking their habitat,
The men killed the poor Florida panther.

Samantha Noelle Atherton (7)
British Embassy Study Group, Turkey

Pollution

P ollution is bad!
O zone we need!
L osing atmosphere,
L osing energy,
U sing too much gas,
T oo much driving,
I don't like it!
O ceans have too much litter,
N o more honking!

Peter Godfrey (8)
British Embassy Study Group, Turkey

Global Warming

Global warming!
The planet is storming!
Heating up, will not stop!
Factories spewing smoke!
Pollution,
The air of Earth is soaked in it!
Only 3000 tigers left in the world!

Global warming has unfurled . . .

Aylin Laity (10)
British Embassy Study Group, Turkey

The Planet Of My Dreams

I wish for a planet with no war,
Let's save our planet from pollution
And animals from extinction.
Come on let's recycle everything.
Avoid global warming.

Berke Nzliaka (8)
British Embassy Study Group, Turkey

Litter Everywhere

Rubbish place,
Scary garbage,
Creating a monster shape,
Hard life and sadness everywhere,
The smell of garbage and dead animals,
Fear is what you can feel,
So tidy up,
And we can live in a clean world.

Bora Sayer (8)
British Embassy Study Group, Turkey

Animal Extinction

People cut off rabbits' feet,
Christians eat pig meat,
Dogs left on the street,
Make the world a better place,
People hurt black bats,
People kill cute rats,
Cut off animals' habitats,
Make the world a better place.

Begum Gürel (8)
British Embassy Study Group, Turkey

Trees

Trees give food,
Trees sparkle in the rain,
Trees bring oxygen outside,
Trees are big plants,
Trees are the home of animals,
Some animals also hide in the trees,
If all trees die, we won't live.

Manul Semtner (8)
British Embassy Study Group, Turkey

Endangered Polar Bears

Polar bears are cute and white,
They are fluffy and academic!
So we must save our world and the polar bears from melting,
Then we must stop doing carbon dioxide and stop the
Hunters making clothes with polar bears' fur,
Then the ice will grow,
Then the polar bears can rest and we can live happily.

Derya Simsek (7)
British Embassy Study Group, Turkey

Pollution Poem

Pollution, what will we do?
Will anyone save me and you?
Not Superman,
Not Batman,
Not even Spider-Man,
You that's who!
You're the one that can save me and you.

Nikki Wright (10)
British Embassy Study Group, Turkey

Wet

Water looks like a pool,
A water's colour is blue, it's like a raindrop
Falling on us from the sky,
A raindrop looks like a water bomb from the sky,
We have to get water for the vegetables,
We have to stop wasting water because we need it,
For our bath and to brush our teeth and to wash everything.

Kemal Akman (7)
British Embassy Study Group, Turkey

A World Of My Extinction

A world of my extinction,
In China I live,
I have no home,
Or bamboo to eat,
Thousands of me lying down,
All in danger, soon hard to be found.

Zeynep Yilal (9)
British Embassy Study Group, Turkey

H²O

Fish are dying,
Dams are getting filthy,
Water has to be clean,
Water is life giving,
Don't waste it.

Niklas Johnson (8)
British Embassy Study Group, Turkey

So This Is What We Do

The bottle is green,
The sky is blue
So what can we do?

You should put bottles in the recycling bin
To keep it clean and clear.
The leaves should go in the brown recycling bin
So the country is clean
For creatures to live, and trees and people.

What can we do to help recycling?
Pick up plastic bottles, things that need recycling.

Lauren Simpson (10)
Christ Church CE Primary School, Birkenhead

Who am I?

Who am I?
I'm blue and green,
You see me from outer space,
I'm round and fat,
Who am I?

Keep me clean and tidy,
Never know what will happen,
Trees will clash,
Cars will smash,
The choice is yours,
Help me!

Who am I?
I have families in me,
From beetles to elephants,
From cats to dogs,
I've had many types of species in me,
Keep me going on.
If you help me,
I'll be here,
If you don't,
I'll disappear.

Ceri Sullivan (11)
Christ Church CE Primary School, Birkenhead

Recycle

R espect the trees and wood
E aten by the birds,
C ut, don't cut our wood,
Y o-yo, made by wood.
C ycle, cycle for our paper,
L eaves grown from a tree,
E verything has gone because we haven't been *recycling*.

Kelsie Day (10)
Christ Church CE Primary School, Birkenhead

Recycling

Recycle, recycle,
Recycle paper,
Recycle things like
Cans and bottles.

Keep our world clean
Put litter in the bin,
Or how about recycling things?

Litter, litter,
Put wrappers in the bin,
Put plastic bags in the bin,
Or maybe paper.

Keep our world clean,
Recycle things, and do what you're told.

Kayleigh Bett (10)
Christ Church CE Primary School, Birkenhead

Imagine

Imagine if the world was full of bad machines,
Would it be right to eat our beans?
Imagine that the people weren't around,
And robots ruled the ground.

Imagine if we threw all the paper away,
And when it came to letters we didn't know what to say.
Imagine if we lived in metal,
Because it was hard to settle.

It doesn't have to be that way,
Only if you hear me say,
Come on and do your bit,
And recycle, you must not sit.

Samantha Murray (10)
Christ Church CE Primary School, Birkenhead

Saving Is Good

Saving is good,
Saving electricity,
Saving water,
Saving light.
So save electric and water and light,
And recycle as well.
Recycling is good.
Recycle bottles, glass, paper, cardboard,
And other things just like that.

Matthew Wheeler (11)
Christ Church CE Primary School, Birkenhead

My Tree

I have a tree that sits in my back garden,
It's been there over 100 years,
It has been loved and cared for.

I wish they would never take it away, it would hurt.
We play games and I sit on his arms,
It's worth 100 dollars.
I love it, I love it, it will never break my heart.

Have you got a tree?

Courtney Guy (10)
Christ Church CE Primary School, Birkenhead

Recycling is Fun

Recycling is fun,
So you can join in too,
Help me send a message
To all my friends and you.

Before we all turn into litterbugs,
This is what we will do,
Help the human race,
Including me and you.

Kevin Day (10)
Christ Church CE Primary School, Birkenhead

Polluting

Polluting can kill us. It can flood a town.
Many people may drown. Death will come quickly.
Unless you decide not to drown,
Use less energy that can save the town.

Save some money and you can walk around,
It's not hard, you're polluting the town.
The town needs you, don't look away and frown!
The world is counting on you to make a difference to Earth.

Charlie Shaw (10)
Christ Church CE Primary School, Birkenhead

Help!

Help us as we all go green,
If you do you will have seen
That this is a friendly place,
And you've saved the human race.

Number one is to recycle bottles, tins and paper,
Even though it seems so hard, you will be so much safer.
Please, please, I'm begging you,
This is easy as steps one and two.

Michelle Olugbode (10)
Christ Church CE Primary School, Birkenhead

Recycle

R ecycle to save our planet!
E ach and everything we recycle helps make *Earth* a better place!
C an you help and save the planet?
Y ou can tell other people to recycle too!
C are about the world!
L et everybody know!
E verybody can save the planet!

Mica Newcomb (10)
Copeland Road Primary School, West Auckland

War And Peace

Love, peace, hope, war,
What is all the fighting for?
Poverty and suffering,
Everyone complaining.
Thought and respect are off the list,
Why do we put up with this?

Milly Armstrong (10)
Copeland Road Primary School, West Auckland

Trees

T he trees are getting cut down to make paper, please recycle,
R ecycle the paper to help the universe.
E lectric wires are going over the forests, and when you cut down the trees, recycle the trees please.
E nvironment needs trees to survive because they breathe oxygen.
S ave the trees from getting cut down to get used for paper.

Luke Berry (10)
Copeland Road Primary School, West Auckland

Trees

T he world needs trees for oxygen,
R ecycle paper, tins, cans, magazines, cardboard and newspaper.
E co-friendly, help others and everyone.
E nergy, don't waste it!
S ave our planet!

Ellie Douthwaite (10)
Copeland Road Primary School, West Auckland

Save Our Seas

S ave our seas, don't put bits of paper in them,
A nd do not put in anything else.
V ery silly people just drop rubbish on sand,
E veryone should put their rubbish in the bin.

O ur planet should be clean for us to live,
U se bins for your rubbish,
R ecycle things like cardboard and cans.

S eas should be safe for fish to live in
E xciting seas for us to swim in.
A lways do the right thing,
S ave the planet by keeping it clean.

Holly McNab (6)
Flora Stevenson Primary School, Edinburgh

Don't Drop Litter

D on't be a litterbug,
O ur world is important,
N ever drop rubbish.
T ry to be eco-friendly.

D on't waste electricity,
R ecycle,
O h! Do not be a litter lout.
P lease reuse.

L ove the world,
I like to reduce, reuse and recycle.
T ry to look after the world.
T ry to keep the world healthy.
E lectricity must be saved,
R espect for the world.

Rebecca Jack (7)
Flora Stevenson Primary School, Edinburgh

Save Our Planet

S ave our planet,
A planet is beautiful,
V ery interesting,
E veryone is helpful to our planet.

O ur planet is great,
U pside down sometimes,
R ecycle.

P eople are in danger,
L ook after the environment,
A lways look after things,
N ature is good for knowing about.
E verybody looking after the world,
T idy your litter.

Maisie Evans (6)
Flora Stevenson Primary School, Edinburgh

Go Green Mad

G reen is cool;
O n the world there is too much rubbish,

G reen is the best!
R educe, reuse, recycle.
E veryone can be green!
E very single one of you, can you be green?
N ever throw rubbish on the floor.

M aybe you can be green,
A dd rubbish *never!*
D on't be mean to the planet, be green.

Jack Bennie (7)
Flora Stevenson Primary School, Edinburgh

On Our Earth

On our Earth there are . . .
Rich people sharing,
But lost children crying.

Wild animals dying
But new trees growing.

Bad people stealing,
But caring people recycling.

I wish everyone was kind.

Maalavisha Sankar (7)
Flora Stevenson Primary School, Edinburgh

Haiku

In Antarctica
The ice is disappearing
Just like a turtle.

David Hale (8)
Flora Stevenson Primary School, Edinburgh

Recycle

R ecycle your rubbish
E at your dinner, don't waste your money,
C ome on, do your job
Y ou have to keep the planet tidy
C an you keep the oceans clean?
L ook after the planet
E xcellent seas to swim in.

Keanna Mair (7)
Flora Stevenson Primary School, Edinburgh

Recycle

R ecycling is good,
E verybody recycle.
C hildren have to recycle,
Y ou are destroying the landscape,
C lean up the environment.
L itter is bad,
E veryone is in it together.

Owen Readman (7)
Flora Stevenson Primary School, Edinburgh

Rules For Recycling

R ules to help save the planet:
E veryone has to have oceans,
C ompost all your fruit skins,
Y ou must save the world.
C ollect cans to recycle,
L itter must always be picked up,
E veryone must do their job.

Ryan Thomas (7)
Flora Stevenson Primary School, Edinburgh

Recycle

R ubbish is bad!
E nvironment is very green.
C hoose if you want to save it or not,
Y es, I love to be green.
C hange our world to a greener world,
L et's help the environment!
E very day you should recycle.

Lisa Gray (7)
Flora Stevenson Primary School, Edinburgh

Recycle

R eturn fish to the sea
E at your food, don't throw it away.
C an you help our world?
Y our help will save our planet
C areful
L ook after our world
E verybody must help.

Max Fleming (7)
Flora Stevenson Primary School, Edinburgh

Litter

L itter is bad,
I have to be green,
T he environment is good,
T o be green is to recycle.
E arth has to be green,
R ubbish isn't good.

Kris Gaff (7)
Flora Stevenson Primary School, Edinburgh

On Our Planet

Lost people disappearing,
Endangered polar bears dying,
Dangerous adults shooting,
Cowardly bullies killing,
Disgusting vandalism growing,
And I want to do something about it.

Shaun McGrath (8)
Flora Stevenson Primary School, Edinburgh

Go Green, Go

L ittering is bad,
I can be green.
T he world needs to be green,
T he environment is good,
E veryone can recycle,
R eady, set, go! We can recycle.

India Lloyd (7)
Flora Stevenson Primary School, Edinburgh

Litter

L itter is dirty,
I t smells.
T here is lots of pollution,
T here are people who want to be green.
E nvironment is good.
R ecycle everything in this world.

Matthew Bagshaw (7)
Flora Stevenson Primary School, Edinburgh

On The Planet - Haiku

The wild animals
Are killed by dangerous men
To make people's coats.

Amelia Mapson (8)
Flora Stevenson Primary School, Edinburgh

Damage

A misty night,
Poppies grow and we wear them
To give peace.

We wear them
And we pay for them,
And we give money to charity.

Battlefields destroyed
And soldiers dying.

Guns shoot, people die
To fight, otherwise
We wouldn't live in a world like this.

Bang, bang, bang,
Shoot, shoot, shoot,
Beware of dynamite and tanks driving over you.

If they didn't fight,
We wouldn't live
In a world like this.

Matthew Price (8)
Great Kingshill CE Combined School, High Wycombe

War

When you're in bed at night
You may feel a fright,
Guns aim, guns shoot
Beware of dynamite.

The navy all in the sea,
Frightening you and me.
Pollution in the air does not seem fair.
RAF soaring in flight.

How many people die?
No wonder people are shy.
All the poppies in the field,
Remind us what they have done,
With their one and only gun.

All the bad stuff in the air,
Makes me think no one cares,
All the oil, the navy leaks,
Surely something bad you see.

Olivia Blake (8)
Great Kingshill CE Combined School, High Wycombe

Save The World

E verything will soon be in danger,
N ow is the time to stop.
V room, the cars racing,
I n every kind of way we kill.
R ecycle,
O h dear, bad pollution.
N ow stop dropping litter,
M elting ice,
E nvironment.
N ever drop litter, find a bin,
T ry to stop.

Myles Stroud (8)
Great Kingshill CE Combined School, High Wycombe

Animals In Danger

A nimals in danger,
N o more to be seen,
I n danger of homes going,
M ankind killing animals.
A giant panda hiding,
L ittle tiger running,
S now leopard terrified.

I n the jungle,
N o more tigers can be seen.

D own in the valley,
A rabian oryx can't be spotted.
N ow do your bit,
G o green,
E veryone,
R euse, reduce, recycle.

Harry Knightley (8)
Great Kingshill CE Combined School, High Wycombe

Don't Drop Litter

If you see litter,
Put it in the bin,
Even if it's you,
Put it in the bin.

Please take care of the world,
Cos it cannot be repaired.
Don't leave anything in the woods
Or animals will die.

Say if glass was dropped,
And a cat came along
And stepped on it,
What would happen next?

Hasan Ishaq (8)
Great Kingshill CE Combined School, High Wycombe

Pollution

When I'm in bed at night
The deadly air begins its flight,
Tapping at the windowpane,
People say it's insane.

I sit by the windowpane
As it carries on through rain,
Pollution, pollution,
Its name is breaking the environment.

You've got to stop this deadly gas
Flying through the air at max,
Pollution, pollution has to stop,
Before the environment is nothing more.

And all the animals have passed away,
Because of that there won't be another day.

Alice Rudkin (8)
Great Kingshill CE Combined School, High Wycombe

Pollution

Don't lose it
If you can reuse it!
Throw it in the bin!
Pollution will win!
Give the world a hand!
It is your land!
Let your goodness shine!
The world will be fine!
The pollution is horrific!
Walk, you'll get a tick!
Don't be mean!
Be green!

Maddy Bridges (8)
Great Kingshill CE Combined School, High Wycombe

Global Warming

Global warming
Is harming our
Environment,
So recycle
Your clothes,
And you won't loathe
The place that you live!

Rushing cars and factories,
Oil spills and exhausts,
'All of these make pollution I see,'
So . . .
Reduce,
Reuse,
Recycle!

Claudia Cook (8)
Great Kingshill CE Combined School, High Wycombe

Environment

E nvironment is important,
N ever ruin it.
V ery important the environment is,
I t is the environment that matters,
R uining it is not good,
O r dropping litter.
N ever spoil it,
M aybe don't do it,
E nvironment gives us air.
N ever destroy the environment,
T ry to stop chucking litter on the floor!

Thomas Lundie-Sadd (8)
Great Kingshill CE Combined School, High Wycombe

Our Environment

Recycle your clothes,
And recycle your glass,
Recycle everything and anywhere.

Our environment needs to be a better place,
The green grass is turning into brown mud,
Our landfill bins are getting full,
So help and recycle your clothes.

You need to help,
Help, help, help,
To recycle your clothes.

Jodie Neal (9)
Great Kingshill CE Combined School, High Wycombe

Litter

Litter is bad,
Litter is horrible,
Litter is nasty,
Litter is evil.

Litter
Can
Destroy
Our
Beautiful
Earth!

Bismah Hussain (9)
Great Kingshill CE Combined School, High Wycombe

Our Environment

Reduce, reuse, recycle,
Don't put it in a landfill.
Reduce, reuse, recycle,
Litter-droppers everywhere.
Reduce, reuse, recycle,
Cars polluting the whole world.
Reduce, reuse, recycle.
Take notice of this poem and you could have a
Nice world to live in.
Reduce - reuse - recycle!

Catriona Roberts (8)
Great Kingshill CE Combined School, High Wycombe

Try To Help

People trying,
Animals crying,
People try,
Animals die.
Why doesn't everyone try?
It would really help,
Animals would live, not die.
And the environment would be better
And safer.

Thomas Williams (9)
Great Kingshill CE Combined School, High Wycombe

Put It In The Bin

If you love animals
Try to think again,
Don't drop litter,
Put it in the bin!

Charlotte Bellamy (8)
Great Kingshill CE Combined School, High Wycombe

Make It A Better World

P ollution can hurt animals,
O nly landfill and litter is dangerous for animals the most.
L andfill isn't good for the Earth.
L itter is better in the bin than on the floor,
U sually it's better to have a clean world.
T alk about putting things in the bin.
I n countries there are people that drop litter on purpose.
O uch, broken glass can hurt.
N ow everyone can see litter everywhere.

Kimberley Rickards (8)
Great Kingshill CE Combined School, High Wycombe

The Rainforest

The rainforest is wild and wet
But still as beautiful as can be,
And is still being harmed,
Just please save the rainforest, please.

The rainforest has some lovely animals,
All big or small,
There's nothing bad about them,
It's just us humans, that's all.

Rachel Stewart (8)
Great Kingshill CE Combined School, High Wycombe

The World Is In Your Hand

Don't drop litter, put it in the bin,
Don't drop litter, put it in the bin.
You could kill an animal,
So put it in the bin.

Lily Hansford (8)
Great Kingshill CE Combined School, High Wycombe

Rainforest Destroyed

Beautiful trees,
Wonderful animals,
Amazing streams,
All about the rainforest.

And then,
It gets ruined,
By us,
For land.

Fintan Jenkinson (8)
Great Kingshill CE Combined School, High Wycombe

It Once Was Green And Beautiful

It once was green and beautiful,
But now it's black and dull,
People just drop their litter,
Like it doesn't matter anymore.

It once was green and beautiful,
 And wasn't polluted like now,
The air is still important,
So we should get people to stop somehow.

Amy Williams
Great Kingshill CE Combined School, High Wycombe

The Recycling Bin

Don't drop litter, put it in the bin,
Keep the wildlife happy and use the recycling bin.
Recycle cans, recycle paper, and plastic bottles too,
Make people happy, do.
Remember, remember the recycling bin,
So if you see rubbish put it in.

Abigail Pinner (8)
Great Kingshill CE Combined School, High Wycombe

Save Our Earth

Save our Earth, save our Earth,
It's not a huge bit of turf.
Save our Earth, save our Earth,
It has been like this since birth.

Save our Earth for the future,
Don't drop litter, put it in the bin.
Save our Earth for the future,
Litter is bad, even an old tin.

Jessica Dixon (9)
Great Kingshill CE Combined School, High Wycombe

Don't Drop It

Don't drop litter,
Put it in the bin.
Don't drop litter,
Put it in the bin.
Keep our country
As tidy as tidy can be.
So don't drop litter,
Put it in the bin!

Robert Smith (8)
Great Kingshill CE Combined School, High Wycombe

Pollution - Haikus

Pollution is bad,
I recycle all the time,
Can you recycle?

Recycle today,
Or your planet will change now,
Recycle always.

Gabbie Fountain (8)
Great Kingshill CE Combined School, High Wycombe

Recycle

R euse clothes,
E xtinction is bad for animals,
C ans, recycle them, don't put them in the bin.
Y ou are harming animals,
C arbon dioxide is needed by the trees,
L andfill is really bad,
E dible things are good, but reuse the packaging after.
Reuse and recycle.

Alexa Tunnicliffe (8)
Great Kingshill CE Combined School, High Wycombe

In The Environment

In the environment
There are men working hard,
In the environment.
There is rubbish lurking in streets,
In the environment.
Animals are dying,
Pollution is going up,
In the environment.

George Keeley (9)
Great Kingshill CE Combined School, High Wycombe

Pollution Is Bad

Pollution causes the environment to die,
Pollution must be bad,
People hate pollution, and so do I.
I hate pollution,
I think it's stupid and mad,
So when I use pollution,
I'm very sad.

James Dixon (9)
Great Kingshill CE Combined School, High Wycombe

Polluting The World!

The Earth is being polluted,
Caused by gases like methane.
If you want to stop it
Then try to think again.
We love our planet dearly,
We really, really do.
So don't drop litter,
Then we might be OK!

Yasmin Richardson (9)
Great Kingshill CE Combined School, High Wycombe

Destroyed - Haikus

I can see the bags
I can smell the leftovers,
I can feel the air.

The world is destroyed,
And packets over the floor,
And the world is full.

Lily Hughes (8)
Great Kingshill CE Combined School, High Wycombe

Pollution Kills

Pollution kills
Babies crying in their beds,
Birds flying and then dying.

I give you a mountain, you give me a cave,
I give you the countryside, you give me houses,
I give you life, you give me guns.

Luke Donnellan
Great Kingshill CE Combined School, High Wycombe

Environment

Reduce, reuse, recycle,
Are the three Rs.
What about pollution that's coming from cars?
What if you lose it, you can't reuse it.
If you love animals try and think again,
Don't drop litter, put it in the bin.

Patrick Orford (8)
Great Kingshill CE Combined School, High Wycombe

Don't Drop Litter

Don't drop litter,
Put it in a bin.
To keep our country as tidy
As 1983.
So don't drop litter,
Put it in a bin!

Max Grimmett (8)
Great Kingshill CE Combined School, High Wycombe

Life Savers

Don't drop litter, put it in the bin,
Don't drop litter, put it in the bin, so
Don't drop litter, put it in the bin, oh
Don't drop litter, put it in the bin.
You could kill an animal,
So don't drop litter, put it in the bin.

Jasper Garofalo (8)
Great Kingshill CE Combined School, High Wycombe

Recycle This

Recycle this, recycle that,
Don't throw it in the bin.
Recycle it, don't be stupid,
It'll go to landfill, you don't want that,
The basic message is:
The world is in your hands.

Eddie Colwill (9)
Great Kingshill CE Combined School, High Wycombe

Litter

L itter is bad,
I don't like it.
T ake litter home, put it in the bin,
T ake litter home to clean it up.
E nvironment is important,
R ats can eat it, so watch out!

Eloise Godfrey (8)
Great Kingshill CE Combined School, High Wycombe

Environment

Environment, environment, it's a lovely place to be,
But some people spoil it by dropping litter
And not putting it in a recycling bin.
A clean place to be is a happy place to be,
Spoilt with rubbish, put it in the bin.
You'll feel good about yourself, I guarantee you will.

Oliver Martins (8)
Great Kingshill CE Combined School, High Wycombe

Environment

The world is so green,
After an hour the world can easily change.
Now it is a horrible smelly place for people,
The children's lives are wrecked.
The ice caps are melting and starting to fall,
It is not a nice place to live in.

Ollie Dixon
Great Kingshill CE Combined School, High Wycombe

Because of Pollution

Because of pollution animals die,
Because of pollution birds can't fly,
Because of pollution the sun's too bright,
Because of pollution nothing has gone right.

Harry King (8)
Great Kingshill CE Combined School, High Wycombe

Don't Drop Litter

Don't drop litter,
Put it in the bin,
If you drop litter,
It really is a sin.

Afsa Hussain (9)
Great Kingshill CE Combined School, High Wycombe

Fairtrade Poem

I work all day long,
I deserve some land,
For my fruit to grow on.
I wish I was in Fairtrade,
To get a decent pay.

If I was in Fairtrade,
I could live in peace,
With electricity and TV.
I would take my children to school,
If I had some money.

I get a fair price now,
I take my children to school now,
I get food now,
And I have a bed now,
Now I am part of Fairtrade!

Ryan Easthaugh
Hartside Primary School, Crook

Fairtrade Poem

I should get some food every day
Fairtrade is most of my day,
Fairtrade is most of my life,
Fairtrade is the best of my life.

Fairtrade means that we are paid
A fair price.
I can't leave Fairtrade behind,
Fairtrade is what we want.

You can get Fairtrade
Every day,
Let's make Fairtrade
Save the day.

Sophie Hauxwell
Hartside Primary School, Crook

Fairtrade Poem

I pick fruit all day,
My children say,
'When are we going to get fed?
And when can we have a comfy bed?'

One day Fairtrade came and rescued me.
Now me and my family are so happy,
We can afford some food and electricity,
And live in peace and harmony.

Now my children can play out,
But I wish we had a
Better place to stay.

Melissa Jones
Hartside Primary School, Crook

Fairtrade Poem

I am a farmer that lives far away,
I work in a country where you don't get much pay,
I grow bananas and tea too.
But my family is poor and I am too.
Oh what should I do?
Oh what should I do?

I've had an idea,
And I hope you have too,
I will join Fairtrade,
And that will make me happy,
Oh yes it will.

Niamh Blackett
Hartside Primary School, Crook

Fairtrade Poem

I pick bananas every day,
But I don't get fairly paid.
I wish I was part of Fairtrade,
Because I need to feed my family,
But I don't have enough food.

My children don't go to school,
And don't get enough sleep.
I am going to try to get to be
A fair trader, so I can buy
Some medicine, and so I can buy more.

Timothy Collyer
Hartside Primary School, Crook

Fairtrade Poem

I pick fruit all day,
My hands start to ache,
I wish
I had good pay.

I pick fruit all day,
My back gives me an ache,
I wish
I was in Fairtrade
So
I could have a lucky break.

Caine Longstaff
Hartside Primary School, Crook

Fairtrade Poem

I should get some food every day,
Fairtrade is most of my day.
Every day it's most of my life,
Fairtrade is the best day of my life.
Fairtrade means that I get paid a fair price,
I can't leave Fairtrade behind.
Fairtrade is what we want,
You can get Fairtrade food every day.
Let's make Fairtrade save the day.

Jasmine Moore
Hartside Primary School, Crook

Fairtrade Poem

I have no name, I live alone,
I have no food so I have to chew a bone.
Eats only once a day,
I have a stack of hay to sleep on.

I grow plants each day and sell
Them for money, so I can buy honey and a bunny.

I love it when it's fair, so let's start
With Fairtrade.

Michael Craggs
Hartside Primary School, Crook

Fairtrade Poem

I pick bananas every day,
But I don't get fairly paid.
I wish I was part of Fairtrade,
Because I need to feed my family.

My children don't go to school,
They get no sleep on the bumpy floor.
Let's make life better,
Let's have Fairtrade.

Rowan Hope
Hartside Primary School, Crook

Fairtrade Poem

I like Fairtrade apples,
They are juicy and delicious,
But I do not think about the
People who have worked
For the apple I am eating.
What an awful life they might have,
Their land could be polluted,
They could be starving.

Ellie McGurk
Hartside Primary School, Crook

Fairtrade Poem

I pick fruit all day,
My back starts to ache,
I wish I got more pay.

I pick fruit all day,
My hands start to ache,
I wish I was in Fairtrade.

Dylan Quinn
Hartside Primary School, Crook

Fairtrade Poem

I pick fruit every day,
My child says,
'When are we going to get fed?
And when are we going to school?'
So everywhere I go I can't find food to eat.
Now I have everything that I need,
Wow, I have me and my family.
Thank you Fairtrade.

Bailey Colman
Hartside Primary School, Crook

Fairtrade Poem

Fairtrade is good and it helps people,
And Fairtrade bananas are nice and fresh,
You can be happy because Fairtrade has come.
People should be fair all the time,
And their houses are bare,
Their kids like Fairtrade apples,
But they don't like pears,
And they don't get a lot of money.

Jack Hodgson
Hartside Primary School, Crook

Fairtrade Poem

I have fruit to pick every day,
And I don't think that's fair,
I don't think my boss cares,
Because I pick a lot of pears.
I don't get a lot of money,
Because I am very poor,
Until *Fairtrade* comes.

Jak Crocher
Hartside Primary School, Crook

Fairtrade Poem

I stay all day in the sun picking fruit,
So I get paid but not enough to have food.

One day in the sun I joined Fairtrade,
Now I have decent pay.

Now I have food to eat and our life has changed,
All because of *Fairtrade!*

Tom Sheppard
Hartside Primary School, Crook

Recycle Bins

In recycle bins we put cans,
Bottles, plastic and wood.
It is a wonderful way
To save the environment.
You can put the stuff in a recycling bag
Without a recycling bin.

The sign is to remind you
To recycle stuff you can.
People who work in a recycling factory
Use a machine.
Recycling is an amazing way
To save the environment.

If the machine doesn't work
They will buy a new one.
If you put in an empty bottle
They will scrunch it up,
And they will take it
To the recycle factory,
And turn it into a new bottle,
Or other stuff.

Mathushan Krishnakumar
Latymer All Saints CE Primary School, Edmonton

Flowers

Flowers, flowers,
They grow so fast.
Smell the sweetness
From the flowers,
Look at the health of the flower,
Look at the way it blooms
Out in the nice hot sun.

Look at the colours on the flowers,
Smell that nectar.
The flower is smooth.
Look at the way the leaves start to sway,
Look at the way the flower grows
Taller and taller.

They grow and grow,
All the leaves start to change
In a different season.
Flowers, flowers, you need sunlight,
You need some air,
You need lots of water.
It is so lonely,
Look at that family of ladybirds.

Rianna Marquis
Latymer All Saints CE Primary School, Edmonton

Litter Is Stinky

L itter is a stinky thing,
I t makes me sad, it makes me unhappy.
T he floor is dirty and I do not like it,
T he litter is causing pollution.
E ars are hearing not to do it,
R ecycle your litter or put it in the bin, that is why it's there.

Promise Emesi (8)
Latymer All Saints CE Primary School, Edmonton

Doves

Doves are beautiful,
Doves are great
With their smooth wings,
They blow you away.
It flies above me
With its enormous wings,
Past the building, past my friends.

Then with its minute feet
It will land on the soft grass
And walk to a tree
To see all its friends,
So that they can fly together
Above the clouds,
Above a tree.

After that its long neck is tired
So it lands again and goes to sleep.
Tomorrow the white feathers
Can shine again.

Dorcas Basia
Latymer All Saints CE Primary School, Edmonton

Flowers

Should I come and smell your nectar?
Or should I come and see
Your colourful petals with a detector?
Or should I sow some seeds
And kill a lot of weeds?
What should I do, my beautiful flower?

Flower, flower,
Can you grow as tall as a tower?

Allysia Cunningham
Latymer All Saints CE Primary School, Edmonton

Pollution

Pollution is disgusting,
Full of poisonous gas,
It smells like horrible dust,
It makes little children cry,
Choked with awful air.

Slowly it comes out of a minute tank
With little square holes.
It makes people cough.
Steam comes out of a factory,
The colour is black.
Smoke comes out creating rotten air.
The air is a killer filled with poisonous gas
And acid rain.

Temi Adegbayibi
Latymer All Saints CE Primary School, Edmonton

The Dove

This dove is kind,
Cute, calm, clean and helpful.
It's singing to me,
It's talking to his/her friends.

The dove is white and it's so right,
It's so calm, smooth, careful and kind.
The dove likes people, it talks to you,
It's enormous, huge, massive.

It has a lovely singing voice,
It's clean, smooth, shy and huge,
The dove is always happy,
It likes everyone.

Seline Ansal
Latymer All Saints CE Primary School, Edmonton

Save The World

We're wasting time,
We've got to save the world.
There ain't much time,
We've got to save the world.

Let's turn off the lights when not needed,
Let's not litter on the pavement,
Let's recycle to save all of our trees,
Let's save the world.

We're wasting time,
We've got to save the world.
There ain't much time,
We've got to save the world.

Godgift Emesi (10)
Latymer All Saints CE Primary School, Edmonton

Rainforests

It is bad to cut and burn the rainforest,
Trees and leaves suck all the carbon dioxide.
Without the trees, the rainforests won't be rainforests,
In time, where the rainforests are will all be houses.

Hugh Paterson (8)
Lochdar School, Lochdar

Hunting

Innocent creatures killed in a second, or maybe blink of the eye,
Gone from the world forever, at least they were not shy!
So bold! So nimble! So quick!
Alone in the day, alone in the night,
People in groups, flying a kite!
Animals dying closer to the river,
Where the young tigers, surely must shudder!
Shooting animals, some nearly gone,
The sun came down so brightly, it shone!
Now to this day, up in the sky,
Most of our birds, slowly fly!
Although there are knives,
Although there are guns,
Why do we kill animals,
And sell their lungs?
The creatures around us could now disappear,
Due to human beings.
Animals locked up in cages,
Now should be sight-seeing.
We can make the world a better place,
So don't let out a yelp!
It only takes a little,
So please, will you help?

Denica Whinn (9)
Lowca Community School, Whitehaven

Litter

Why drop litter, why?
Why not use a bin, why?
Why let litter pickers do your job, why?
The world looks appalling with litter dropped,
Why drop litter, why?
Litter attracts rats,
Oh, litter attracts rats.
Do you like to damage the world?
Because if you drop litter, you are,
You are being careless,
You are being appalling.
This is not a caretaker's job,
It is yours!
Do your job!
Don't be cruel.
You can make a difference,
Oh, do your job!
Don't be cruel!
You can really make a difference!

Luke Johnston (10)
Lowca Community School, Whitehaven

Air Killers

What is wrong with our world?
Pollution's taken over,
All the animals are dying,
And plants are too like clover.

It's very careless of people,
Setting off this gas,
If we keep on like this
Our environment won't last.

Since when did the world change?
How did it happen?
And please tell me who's responsible,
I'm gonna slap 'em.

What are people breathing in?
It's from the air,
Hey now, what about you?
Do you really care?

Jason Fleming (11)
Lowca Community School, Whitehaven

Killing Animals Is Not Good

Do you want to kill animals?
Do you think it is good?
Hunters kill little babies,
And put them in their hoods.
There were at least fifteen that died a day.

In this world we have none left, hardly,
We have got tigers and elephants,
Some cheetahs too.

Stop killing them now,
Do you want each animal to vanish?
We want to save them not kill them, do you?

Megan Foster (10)
Lowca Community School, Whitehaven

Planetary Pollution

Factories and car fumes,
Manufacturers and such,
They're polluting our air,
It's a bit too much.

What has happened to all the green leaves?
Those manufacturers stole them,
With their huge factories,
They are such great thieves.

We can help save the Earth,
We need to get those idiotic
Manufacturers off our turf,
Or face them head first.

Do you think that
They will ever quit?
Please tell me now,
They need a good hit.

Jake Martin (11)
Lowca Community School, Whitehaven

Don't Kill Sharks!

Why kill sharks?
Why kill creatures?
Why not take the time to read the features?

Sharks are vicious,
But aren't they cute,
And that big thing that is staring at it is a . . .
Giant newt.

Sharks are famous,
Sharks are massive,
But sharks can be,
Over-reactive.

Charlie Walker (10)
Lowca Community School, Whitehaven

Animal Hunting

Do you care about the deer?
Can't you see they're in fear?
Why are you killing them?
Can't you see you're hurting them?
You're even killing a little stoat.
Deer are lovely to see,
So don't eat them for tea.
Do you care about us?
You're nearly killing us.
Don't let much out,
You'll kill agent Mount.
Do you care about plants?
You're killing all the ants,
Do you care about flowers?
You're killing them all with your powers.

Leona Jolly (9)
Lowca Community School, Whitehaven

Trees

Why are trees being cut down?
Do we need to cut them down?
'Cut them down, make room for homes!'
Thousands of protests every day.
'Don't do it! Don't do it!'
Recycle! Recycle!
The headline says
Nobody listens though,
Even the wood animals are nearly gone.
Once there were lots on the beautiful
Earth, all covered in trees.
Now, oh, now there have been many lost.

So, why are trees being cut down?

Rebecca Iredale (9)
Lowca Community School, Whitehaven

Hunting Will Be Banned

Why do they kill tigers?
They could halt it now!
But ignorance, and greed is ahead.
Could any innocent take a bow?
Tigers are decreasing,
And can't escape the cell.

Sometimes they starve!
They cannot ring that bell.
Why do they kill tigers?
They'll only end up in Hell!

Hunting will be banned,
Hunting shall be over,
Hunters = losers.
Why do they kill tigers?

Marcus Maudlin (9)
Lowca Community School, Whitehaven

Animals Are Going Extinct

People are running over frogs and animals for no point at all,
Would you like it if you were that helpless animal?

Our animals are going extinct.
Our world is running out of creatures.
Our place where we live has endangered species here.
Our life, is it all about killing them for no point?

Stop running over animals, make the world a better place.
Stop shooting animals with guns or bows and arrows.
Stop hunting where endangered species live.
Stop shooting them out of trees.

Now!

Jessica Johnston (10)
Lowca Community School, Whitehaven

Hunters

Terrific tigers,
Rapid cheetahs,
Cheeky monkeys,
Sneaky leopards,
Tall deer,
Slow elephants,
Crazy rhinos,
Lazy hippos,
Wild lions,
Small pandas,
Do you like these animals dead?

James McNally (10)
Lowca Community School, Whitehaven

Why Do People Hunt Such Sweet Animals?

Why do people hunt such sweet animals
Like monkeys, deer, tigers, lions,
Cheetahs and chimps?
And hunting is wrong,
For fun and money,
It is cruel.
They become extinct.
And I think people from the government
Should ban all hunting,
And shut all the gun shops and knife shops,
So please don't hunt.

Jordan Hetherington (9)
Lowca Community School, Whitehaven

Animals In Danger

Do not kill animals.
If you see an animal
And you are scared
Of it, do not kill it.
Animals that can be
In danger are tigers
And giant pandas.
If someone tries to
Kill them there will not
Be any more of them
Because in your whole
Life there are two of them,
Two have gone no more.
Try saving them instead
Of killing them,
Then you feel what you
Have done, and it is not a
Nice thing that you have
Done.

Maliha Ahmed (8)
Manchester Muslim Preparatory School, Withington

Animals and Extinction

Animals are becoming extinct,
Because people are killing them.
Animals' habitats are getting destroyed,
Different animals are getting killed.
Elephants are becoming extinct
Because of their horns and meat.
Animals are becoming extinct,
Because their habitats are getting destroyed,
Taken over by hunters.
Help them survive.

Umar Rashid (8)
Manchester Muslim Preparatory School, Withington

Here Is The Terrible War

In war everything is rationed,
In war you hear the distracting siren,
In war you need to be safe from the chilli bombs,
In war it is red of blood,
In war it is destroying places,
In war never waste food.
It will have to stop now.
War is a very mean thing to do,
Bye-bye war.

In war you have very little clothes,
In war listen carefully for the siren,
In war never forget there is a war on.
In war never forget there is no electricity,
In war wake up at night and go in the air raid shelter.
In war, remember your dad.
It will have to stop now.
War is a mean thing to do,
Bye-bye war.

Saarah Choudary (8)
Manchester Muslim Preparatory School, Withington

Litter

Litter is bitter.
It is old and will turn into mould.
If you throw litter it will kill the plants and things in it, like ants.
If you throw litter you are bad,
And it makes people who recycle sad.

So be a good lad, recycle,
And don't be too slow to recycle something heavy.
Recycle metal from a broken kettle.
Recycle to save the world.

Seif Mohammed (9)
Manchester Muslim Preparatory School, Withington

Recycle

Always recycle, never waste,
Recycle paper, recycle glass, recycle cans
And recycle everything else that you can.
Don't be silly, and put your stuff in the bin,
Put it in the recycling bin.

Don't put your food in the bin, give it away to someone,
If you are silly you would put your paper in the bin,
If not, put it in the recycling bin.
Don't waste water and put it down the drain, drink it.

If you have any small clothes, don't put them in the bin,
Give them to your sister.
If you have an empty tissue tube, don't put it in the bin,
Make it into something special that is thin.
Recycle, recycle, never waste,
Because it would be such a shame.

Alani Anazim (8)
Manchester Muslim Preparatory School, Withington

Recycle, Recycle

R ecycle, recycle.
E leven egg shells.
C lever Chloe recycles cardboard.
Y oung Yasmin recycles shoes.
C lever Calum recycles paper.
L ittle Lee recycles fabric.
E verything can be recycled.

You see even you can recycle jars,
And you can recycle parts of cars.
You can recycle crisp packets,
Even your blue jackets.
Everything can be recycled.

Faiz Mohammed (8)
Manchester Muslim Preparatory School, Withington

Recycle

Paper, plastic and glass
Are all the things you could be recycling.
If you recycle paper
You will save the trees.
If you save the trees you save the bees.
You can walk to school
To save the environment.
Don't waste water because
There will be a flood.
Always turn the lights off
Or you will waste a lot
Of electricity.
Recycle plastic, paper, glass
And some cans, and you will
Be a recycling star.

Talha Khan (9)
Manchester Muslim Preparatory School, Withington

War

War is bad, war is sad,
Homes destroyed,
Cries and tears.
I don't know why,
Land's destroyed.
Why?
Evil nations and good nations,
And crime, diseases, poor people
Sitting on the street,
Looking for food to eat,
And
Why does it have to be?
The sign
Of war.

Hamza Haq (8)
Manchester Muslim Preparatory School, Withington

Recycle

Recycle food, bicycles, paper and a car.
Everyone should, from here to far.

Save electricity, animals, water and trees,
Recycle with a lot of ease.

Don't smoke and don't waste,
Recycle bottles, cans and food you don't want to taste.

Walk to school, do not drive,
When you go swimming you can dive.

Recycle, don't waste,
And make the world a better place.

Aqsa Saied (9)
Manchester Muslim Preparatory School, Withington

Recycle

Paper, plastic and a tin can is all you need for a recycling plan.
If you litter, instead of recycling, you will need a babysitter.
Don't waste water
Because you will set a bad example for your daughter.
Save the trees and the bees.
Recycle a plastic bag and you won't hear your mum nag.
Walk to school and then you can talk to school.
If you recycle metal then you are a star petal.

Amirah Mohammed (8)
Manchester Muslim Preparatory School, Withington

War

War is not good
Because all you can hear is shoot, shoot.
People are dying,
Please don't encourage
Because it is not good, this is not fun.
The world is raiding,
The war has not stopped.
The knife costs somebody's life.

Yusuf Mahmoud (8)
Manchester Muslim Preparatory School, Withington

Recycle

R ecycle to save the environment,
E veryone remember to turn the lights off.
C lever people recycle compost.
Y ou can recycle cans, paper and plastic too.
C ool people always take care,
L eaving litter is a hazard.
E njoy the world around you.

Subaat Rathur (8)
Manchester Muslim Preparatory School, Withington

Homeless

Nothing to eat in the heat.
You have to live on the street with your bare feet.
Give some meat for them to eat.
Being homeless isn't good,
You don't have a wood to sleep on.
You can't believe what they need.

Faris Akhtar (8)
Manchester Muslim Preparatory School, Withington

Bullying

Bully:
I yell out to a boy for him to come to me,
How dare he say no to me, the best bully on Earth?
I kick him on the chest and he falls on the floor,
I then poke him on the tooth and blood starts to gush.
I clip his ears with my scissors and he cries in pain,
Then I shove him on my bike and ride him to an empty bin,
I shove him in, close the lid and run.
I yell out to him, 'This is what happens
When you say no to a bully,' and add an evil laugh.

Victim:
I sneak out of the school
Slowly keeping a look out for Billy the bully.
I scan the playground looking for a place to hide.
I find one and go there, but Billy gets me,
He gave me a punch, so I gave him my lunch.
I can't think what will happen tomorrow in the killing ground.

Avi Garson (9)
Pardes House Primary School, Finchley

Victim's Poem

I stand very scared,
I want to be spared.
I feel someone punch me in the back,
'Please don't whack.'
He says, 'Just get out of here.'
Next time I am going to fear.

Motti Stern (10)
Pardes House Primary School, Finchley

Bullying

Bully:
I slouch against the wall
Waiting for my tiny victim.
I feel like a tiger waiting for its meat,
'Come here little frog,' I growl.
I chased him and boxed him in the eye,
I feel very happy like a king who has money.

Victim:
I came outside as white as a sheep,
I stand like a straight pole,
I feel like a scaredy cat.
I mumbled to myself, 'This is the end.'
He chased me and boxed me in the eye,
I feel scared and worried thinking, 'What will
Happen tomorrow in the killing ground?'

Motty Sprung (9)
Pardes House Primary School, Finchley

Bullying

Bully:
I stood as strong as a lion,
I was growling with anger,
I felt like I was gonna smash him up.
I warned, 'Don't mess with me because I will smash you up!'
Then I threw him down on the whole playground.

Victim:
I stood shivering, as frightened as a chicken,
I snuck down the playground,
I was frightened because I thought they would find me.
'Please don't hurt me,' I yelled,
He forced me to give him money.
I felt so ashamed.

Modchele Kahan (10)
Pardes House Primary School, Finchley

Bullying

Bully:
I stared at a cute little boy,
I chased him a mile away,
I felt as strong as a lion.
I said, 'Who wants to start with me?'
I grabbed another victim,
I felt powerful and strong.

Victim:
I crept to the nearest hiding place so I won't be caught,
I begged for mercy, but the bully didn't listen to me,
I felt broken-hearted, and I called,
'Help, help, I don't have anything to give you.'
The bully chased me a mile away,
I felt like a little piece of rubbish.

Pinchos Dunner (9)
Pardes House Primary School, Finchley

Bullying Poem

Bully:
I stood as strong as a lion,
Clenching my fists aside,
I felt angry throughout my body,
'Get away from me,' I shouted,
Scaring a boy shorter than I.
I felt as if he'd just died.

Victim:
I moved
 backwards, and cowered like a mouse,
I fell down on the ground, shivering like a baby.
I stared and started to cry.
'Stop,' I screamed, looking up at a bully,
I felt like he was the meanest boy in the world.

Dovy Palmer (9)
Pardes House Primary School, Finchley

The Big Green Environment

Our environment is the world to us,
Our land is green like a runner bean,
The ocean has its staring eyes.
We need to save our planet by closing the taps,
Turning lights off, stop leaving technology on standby.

Litter on the pavement and the bags upon the beach,
This is not what we want to see.
So we need to clear up the pavement
And the bags on the beach.
This is what we want to see.

Fossil fuels are running out
So we need to sort this out.
Recycling is a great thing to do,
Recycling more is better for us.
You might think it's boring, but actually
You're saving the whole world,
And our jobs are easier!

Rosy Dias (10)
Priory Primary School, Hull

Everybody Go Green!

Recycle, recycle, everybody recycle,
Bicycle, bicycle, everybody bicycle,

Fossil fuels, fossil fuels, everybody's fossil fuels.
Pollution, pollution, everybody's pollution,

Rainforest, rainforest, everybody's rainforest.
Environment, environment, everybody's environment,

Global warming, global warming, everybody's global warming.
Solar energy, solar energy, everybody's solar energy.

Walk to school, walk to school, everybody walk to school,
Wind turbines, wind turbines, everybody's wind turbines.

Chloe Corlass (10)
Priory Primary School, Hull

The Green Machine Rap!

Now listen to my rap, to make the world a better place,
And before you know it you'll have a smile upon your face.
Just follow these instructions, fit them in the routine,
'Cause you're already looking like healthy kings and queens.

Step 1
Run or walk, don't you dare go by car,
Or ride a bike if it's a bit too far.

Step 2
Recycle card, paper and plastic bags,
Look for the green bin to put all your clothes tags,

And last but not least it's the big *step 3!*
You've got to turn off your electricity,
But don't go round turning everything off,
Be sensible about it, unlike Uncle Bob.

So now you know exactly what to do,
Save the environment and have loads of fun too!

Georgia Green (10)
Priory Primary School, Hull

Pollution Is Bad

The environment is getting worse,
If we carry on the way we're gong
Our world will be a curse.
Our world is full of pollution
So we need to find a good solution.
We recycle as much as we can,
But a lot of people aren't a good fan.
We need to try and make an act,
Or we'll have a big impact.
We need to start using aluminium,
And ask for some people's opinions.

Thomas Gleadhill (10)
Priory Primary School, Hull

Come On!

Animals crying,
Planes are flying,
Loving plants are always dying.

Respect to the world,
And the air,
Stop using cars,
Instead, walk there.

The future is coming,
Get out of bed,
Go help out.
Soon you'll be dead.

Recycle glass, tins and bottles,
Go and tell it,
Go and sell it,
You big green machine!

Declan Hall (10)
Priory Primary School, Hull

The Big Green Future

People chopping down big green trees,
Watching falling lifeless leaves.
Seeing scattered rubbish in the town,
Park owners with big sad frowns.
Why not walk instead of car?
You might not realise, but you will go very far.
Children stuck inside for hours,
You can help with a bit of power.
To do this it will not take a lot,
It's worth every single minute of the plot.
Do this and you won't delay,
The big green future is at pay.

Bethany Soulsby (11)
Priory Primary School, Hull

If The . . .

If the trees could talk they would be saying,
'Don't cut me down.'
If the drink bottle cans could talk they would be saying,
'Recycle me.'
If fossil fuels could talk they would be saying,
'Use something else, we're delicate.'
If the Earth could talk it would be saying,
'Get this cloud off me.'
If the air could talk it would be saying,
'I'm getting a virus from all this pollution.'
If cars could talk they would be saying,
'Get out of me and walk, you lazy things.'
If wind turbines could talk they would be saying,
'I wish I could stop moving - once in a while.'
If the future could talk it would be saying,
'I am coming, so get ready.'

Joshua Streets-Wray (10)
Priory Primary School, Hull

The Green Machine

Our Earth needs to be green,
Just like a runner bean,
So just listen to my poem,
So you can make the world a better place.
And soon you will have a smiley face.
Recycling card, paper and plastic bags,
Put things in the bin, like clothes tags.
Use solar panels to make energy,
And wind turbines to make more,
This should clearly be the law.
If everyone does this,
We can all give the world a great big kiss!

Charlotte Briggs (11)
Priory Primary School, Hull

The Eco Project

Be green, recycle,
Don't go in the car, cycle.
Please give your clothes away,
Put them in the bin, no way.
The environment is a special place,
So if you throw your rubbish
You're a disgrace.
For the subject of pollution,
We're starting to get a solution,
Try to recycle quite a lot,
If you don't, you've lost the plot.
Try not to use fossil fuels,
Because they're just like jewels.
Being eco is important to me,
It's even better than the sea.
So save the environment!

Alex Jenkins (10)
Priory Primary School, Hull

Environment

If you recycle we could have a life cycle,
If we save the plants and trees we save ourselves,
So stop polluting the Earth and stop global warming,
Global warming is like a smashed mirror, bad luck.
When we stop pollution of the Earth
We can live in a better world
And save the environment.
The sun is making us too hot, just like a hot dog,
Wind turbines are helping get electricity,
Which we are wasting, so stop wasting electricity.
Save the environment.

Liam Old (10)
Priory Primary School, Hull

Go Green

It's just like a puzzle,
Can't you see.
The world is getting in a puzzle
Because of the pollution everywhere
In your garden,
Even in the air.
Throwing rubbish, driving cars,
This is what makes the Earth like Mars,
Hot and sandy, nothing really there,
And no people living there.
Do you want Earth to be
Just like Mercury, Venus and Mars?
We don't,
You don't,
They don't,
So go green.

Laura Fee (10)
Priory Primary School, Hull

It's A Green Life

Recycling is important, just you wait and see.
Recycling is important to save the land and sea,
The Earth is important, the birds, the animals mainly,
So do your thing, recycle insanely.
Wind turbines produce energy,
Another way to save the galaxy.
Pollution is bad in every way,
So don't do it, even morning and day.
Always throw paper and cans away!
Remember, be green.

Matthew Robinson (11)
Priory Primary School, Hull

Earth's Environment

Earth has just been polluted,
Save the world by turning off light,
Use as much as possible natural light,
Recycle the drinks we drink,
Then our Earth is saved.

Make me want to live in this place,
Have you got the brains to live?
Use your brains to walk to school,
Rather than drive to school.
Shivers in the dark stormy night,
It's just like 'I'm A Celebrity, Get Me Out Of Here!'

Our environment is the world to us,
Oceans have got its glaring eyes.
Litter on the pavement, bags upon the beach,
This is not what we want to see.

Halil Onay (10)
Priory Primary School, Hull

The Green Environment

Green green grass,
Is something you can pass,
The smooth stalks,
Look like they can talk,
They look like they can really dance,
Then start to puff and pant.

This poem really just isn't about green green grass.
It's about people walking places,
At their own paces.
Think about all the trees,
That you cannot see,
All because of chopping down,
All the trees around town.

Leonie Wright (10)
Priory Primary School, Hull

Environment

Our world is a great place to be,
Especially when we treat it right.

But those who don't treat it right
Might be destroying the Earth.
Quite bad.

By not walking and taking a car
You're sending clouds into the sky,
And that makes the sun reflect
Back down on the Earth, and
Makes the icebergs fall into the
Sea, and makes the water to rise,
And it could flood us.

So think about when you need
Something with gas.

Charlie Sommerville (10)
Priory Primary School, Hull

Our Environment Poem

All the grass that we walk past dies
Of rubbish, and our trash,
Our environments are like a landfill,
We need to be careful where we put rubbish.

We need to look out where we put trash
Or we might make a smash.
We can't keep making the world look like this,
So let's be careful before we go to sleep.

We can help make this world look nice,
If we stop making rubbish and put it in a pack.
We need to watch out in our life,
This is where we live and it won't look nice
If there's trash all over the world!

Jessica Mason (10)
Priory Primary School, Hull

Warning!

Green rainforests,
Pouring with rain,
Let's save the environment for the future.
Carbon monoxide makes clouds,
So try to walk!
Solar energy works with light,
Sometimes it will be bright.,
Wind turbines spin away,
As clouds start to fade away.
Green bins are very good,
Instead of throwing rubbish in a mood.
Pollution is wrecking our world,
Gases have twirled.
If we don't do anything
The world will break in half!

Joshua Iles-Caville (11)
Priory Primary School, Hull

Environment

Our world is a good place to live in
But it needs some tidying up to do.
There are some lazy people
That can't be bothered to put their rubbish in the bin,
They are destroying the world by littering,
So if we treat the world properly it will be a good place.
Save the environment,
Be green, save the world.

Jake Cooper (10)
Priory Primary School, Hull

The Big Green Poem Machine

The environment is good, the environment,
Causing gases and pollution is what we hate.
Walk, run or cycle.
Look at the world, it needs more care,
Finding wildlife could very soon be near,
Look at the world this could be,
If we all recycle we'll be so happy.
Lots of people inhale bad gases,
That's why the government set up classes.
Gases can cause really bad things,
Maybe the hospital doorbell rings.
Most gases have impact,
Pollution is bad, that's a fact.
Really, really bad pollution,
Now it's time to make a solution.

Max Palmer (11)
Priory Primary School, Hull

The Big Green Poetry Machine

Help global warming, recycle stuff, it helps . . .
Animals are dying and plants are trying to stay alive.
Air is flowing, gas is getting thrown into it.
Use a bus, save the pollution,
Use special recycle bins.
Forests are losing all their trees,
We all need to save energy and turn plugs off,
It will save fossil fuels.

Courtney Ferrie (10)
Priory Primary School, Hull

The Big Green Poetry Machine

Have you heard of global warming?
Do you think it's cosy and warming?
Help polar bears to live their lives,
Don't use things that will melt their ice.
Would you live as a polar bear?
Will it give you quite a scare?

Shannon Brinkley (10)
Priory Primary School, Hull

Eco Anthology

Stripes

Stripes in the night,
Glowing green eyes,
Sharp white claws,
Soft smooth skin.

Tiger, tiger in the zoo,
Nowhere else is left for you.
Tiger, tiger who are you?
You're forgotten, left and extinct.

Stomp!

Grey rough skin,
Big floppy ears,
Long powerful trunk,
Strong white tusks.

Elephant, elephant in the zoo,
Nowhere in the wild left for you.
Trees cut down, forests burnt to dust,
Poached for your ivory tusks.
Now all that is left of you are pictures in books.

Bethan Cooper (10)
Rector Drew School, Hawarden

Recycle

The blue bin is for the paper,
The brown bin is for garden waste,
So come on everybody, recycle, recycle, recycle.

Don't throw your rubbish on the floor,
Just recycle that little bit more.

The blue bin is for the paper,
The brown bin is for the garden waste,
So come on everybody, recycle, recycle, recycle.

If you don't recycle, the world will end,
And won't that drive you round the bend.

The blue bin is for the paper,
The brown bin is for garden waste,
So come on everybody, recycle, recycle, recycle.

We can recycle lots of things,
Like paper, cans and tins.

The blue bin is for the paper,
The brown bin is for garden waste,
So come on everybody, recycle, recycle, recycle.

To help the world that little bit more,
Just recycle, recycle, recycle.

**Megan Elizabeth Rowlands, Eithne Preece (10)
& Lauren Jones (11)**
Rector Drew School, Hawarden

Recycle Paper And Throw Litter Away

Recycle paper and throw litter away,
Pick up litter and put it in the bin.
If you recycle paper, plastic and other things
You will save our environment,
And keep it nice and clean.

Kate Newby (7)
Rector Drew School, Hawarden

Save Our Planet

The scientists are kicking up a storm,
They are telling us to beware,
The Earth is getting warm,
But no one seems to care.

The ozone is getting thinner,
Emissions are ever greater.
There can be no winner,
We are losing our Equator.

The ice caps could be lost,
The rainforests too,
At what greater cost
To me and you?

We can turn this round
If we work together,
Solutions can be found,
To solve this now, forever.

Tom Williams (10)
Rector Drew School, Hawarden

My Earth

E verybody should pick litter every day.
N ever dump litter.
V andalism is very bad.
I ce caps can melt.
R ecycle every day.
O xygen comes from trees.
N ever drop litter.
M any people put litter in the bin.
E verybody should recycle.
N ever chop trees down.
T oxic waste is bad.

Katie McLoughlin (8)
Rector Drew School, Hawarden

The Recycle Bin

Wherever you be, please look for me,
I'm tall and thin, I'm the recycle bin.

I'm always happy, never dull, I'm always hungry, never full,
Feed me plenty every day, and by your house I will stay.

Feed me plastic, it tastes fantastic,
I'll chew it slowly so I don't get poorly.

Please don't hoard your old cardboard,
Pop it in me, I'll be as happy as can be.

As for wood, it tastes so good,
I'll munch and crunch from breakfast to lunch.

Empty tin cans, and old metal pans,
Place inside me, these items, you see.

I like glass the best, it outshines the rest,
From bottle to jar, it's my favourite by far.

Jennifer Blythe (10)
Rector Drew School, Hawarden

Eco-Friendly

Recycle your packaging during the day,
Bottles and cans and newspapers too!
We must all be keen
And try to be green.

Turn off the taps when brushing your teeth,
Leave your car at home and go for a walk on the heath.
We must all be keen
And try to be green.

Turn the heating and lights down low at night,
Save on the energy and be green alright!
We must all be keen
And try to be green.

Abi Shevlin (9)
Rector Drew School, Hawarden

Do Your Bit

Think of the polar bears
Running out of ice.
Or think of the litter,
It's not nice.

So do a bit
Or do some more,
You know what it
Is helping for.

We've got to help
And do our thing,
We want to make
The birdies sing.

Megan Rendle (10)
Rector Drew School, Hawarden

Help Our Universe

Reduce, reuse, recycle,
Switch lights off,
Stop wasting.
Save our environment and save our world,

Keep our environment nice and green
By using the Big Green Machine.
Don't forget you have legs and feet,
So don't sit down in the car seat.

Reduce, reuse, recycle,
Switch lights off,
Stop wasting.
Save our environment.

Madeleine Dibble (8)
Rector Drew School, Hawarden

Don't Stand By

What can we do to be more green?
Turn off the light
And heat off at night,
Just *don't stand by!*

What can we do to be more green?
Travel by boat, don't fly,
And choose low energy lights,
Just *don't stand by!*

What can we do to be more green?
Have a shower, not a bath.
Recycle that trash,
Just *don't stand by!*

Edward Williams (10)
Rector Drew School, Hawarden

Make A Change

Trees are getting chopped down, you hear the crunch sound.
The climate is changing because we throw things on the ground.
People are dying of diseases, they can't take anymore.
There's no peace in the world, all because of war.
There are no homes for people, or even the polar bear.
But we don't take an interest, we don't even care.

So recycle your plastic bottles, glasses and tins
By making sure you put them in the correct recycle bins.
Just try and do your best, you don't even have to walk far,
But make a serious effort to not always drive a car.

So have a think, all these things you can rearrange,
Please try to help, you really can make a change.

Charlotte Naylor (10)
Rector Drew School, Hawarden

The Earth's Environment

E veryone should walk to school,
N iamh, my friend, said walking's cool.
V andalism makes the world ill,
I think it should take a really big pill.
R ecycle one thing a day,
O r maybe two, the binmen will pray,
N ow try three.
M um, this morning, cut down a tree,
E veryone saw it, it was really bad.
N ever, ever do it,
T hen you'll be glad.

Jenny Hughes (8)
Rector Drew School, Hawarden

My Earth

E nvironment needs protecting,
N o one dump litter,
V andalism is very bad,
I ce caps are melting.
R ecycle paper and bottles,
O xygen is running out.
N oise pollution is killing the world,
M ore landfill makes the world smelly.
E veryone should reuse,
N ever chop trees down,
T oxic waste is bad.

Tom Kennedy (8)
Rector Drew School, Hawarden

Environment Poem

E very day we should recycle,
N ow the world is in danger.
V andalising should not be done,
I n the world people throw litter.
R educe all the greenhouse gases,
O xygen, plants breathe out, please don't cut them down!
N ow ice caps are melting. That's a bad thing.
M ost people recycle. That's good.
E ven if we get rid of cars that's a big difference.
N o more landfill!
T ry your best to look after the environment. Please!

Adam Brooke-Jones (8)
Rector Drew School, Hawarden

Environment

E nvironment needs trees.
N ever stand on flowers.
V andalism damages the world.
I ce caps are melting.
R ecycle everything we can.
O xygen comes from trees.
N ever waste water.
M ost of us don't care if we kill animals.
E lectricity is wasted.
N oise affects the world.
T oxic waste is bad.

Liam Collins (8)
Rector Drew School, Hawarden

Think Twice

The polar bears are dying, there is no ice,
The way things are going you'd better think twice,
The climate is changing, we need to take care,
How are we going to protect the polar bear?
So recycle more, get out of your car, hop on your bike
And ride as much as you like.

Rainforests are disappearing because we use the wood,
Use an alternative, we really should.
Don't change your furniture just because you change your mind
Think once, think twice, recycle, rewind.

Michael Warrenger (10)
Rector Drew School, Hawarden

Don't Be A Litterbug

Be wise and caring,
It's our world we are sharing.
It makes me feel bitter
When you throw down your litter.
Our Earth won't last long
If you keep doing it wrong.
We can all help to win
By putting rubbish in the bin,
We can make our planet a nicer place,
We can put a smile on everyone's face.

Lucy Harrison (7)
Rector Drew School, Hawarden

How To Save The World

Collect all your tins
And put them in the recycling bins,
Save all your old paper,
It will make the world safer.
Recycle your glass,
(And save on the trash!)
Keep your card,
It's not so hard.
So don't act in haste,
Think before you waste.

Thomas Janney (10)
Rector Drew School, Hawarden

Litter, You And Me

Litter comes from you and me dropping wrappers,
Packets, bottles, that could end up in the sea,
Causing damage to you and me.

Litter can be very harmful to you and me,
And all God's creatures, as you can see.
Litter can hurt the world, fish and birds, and you and me.

Litter can cause disease, danger and harm to you and me,
So please be careful, don't drop litter,
Pick it up, you and me.

Zoe Watson (8)
Rector Drew School, Hawarden

Help Our World!

Recycle, recycle,
That is what we need,
Old tin cans, pick them up please.

Bottles and jars can all be reused,
Don't forget to separate them
From your refuse.

Cardboard boxes and newspapers too,
Help save the planet
For me and for you.

Charlotte Anderton (9)
Rector Drew School, Hawarden

Save Our World

If you don't pick up litter, people will feel bitter,
If you don't want to cycle, just try to recycle.
If you don't switch off lights you will have a power cut at night.
Don't use cars, use your feet.

I have a wonderful solution, let's stop pollution,
Let's save our world, save our world, save our world.
Let's stop war so we can have peace for evermore,
So let's save our world, save our world,
Please help, thank you.

Hannah Baker (8)
Rector Drew School, Hawarden

Save Our World

If we keep on saving water,
People shall stop craving water,
But because we keep on throwing litter,
People feel bitter.

So when you go out of the room
Turn off the lights and don't be afraid of the gloom,
Electricity is valuable, so don't waste it.
So stop declaring war and let's have peace for evermore.
So save our world.

Eleanor Crawford (8)
Rector Drew School, Hawarden

Saving Our World

Save our energy, switch off your light,
Switch off your appliances when you go to bed at night.

Let's leave the car and walk to school,
Use your bike more and use your car less, you fool!

Recycle, reuse, reduce, and use your bin less,
But pick up your rubbish and stop making a mess.

Our world is a beautiful place, keep it that way,
Or we will all end up having to pay.

Michael Preston (10)
Rector Drew School, Hawarden

Save The Environment

Save the planet, save the world,
Switch the light to make the world more bright,
Don't use a car, it leaves pollution.
Walking is the answer to a celebration,
If you don't pick up litter, people will feel bitter,
Pollution isn't the solution.
Please reuse, and remember to pull out the fuse,
If you admit climate change you might even get put in a cage,
So please, please, please make a difference.

Harrison Hayes (8)
Rector Drew School, Hawarden

Save The Planet

Litter, litter, everywhere,
People throw it and just don't care.
Bin it, bag it, all the time,
Chucking rubbish is a crime.
The big blue bag is there for you,
If you chuck, it will not do.
Save the environment,
We all do the same,
Then our planet will be green again.

Louis Kennedy (10)
Rector Drew School, Hawarden

Let's Care For Our Planet

On Wednesday we put out our recycling bins,
That contain glass, paper, plastic and tins.
In amongst the compost waiting to rot,
The insects and bugs are snug and hot.

We help the planet when we recycle our things,
Clothes, cardboard, shoes and toys,
Will bring lots of joy
To girls and boys.

Jack Baker (11)
Rector Drew School, Hawarden

The Environment

The polar bears are losing ice,
Believe me, it isn't nice.
Stop throwing your litter on the floor,
We don't want it anymore.

Cutting down the rainforests is very serious
For the people and animals, it's very dangerous.
We want to make a difference now,
It's up to us to work out how.

Polly Keeling (11)
Rector Drew School, Hawarden

Litterbug

Don't be a litterbug,
Be a litter picker.
Keep the country clean and tidy,
And keep our towns litter-free.
So *don't* be a litterbug,
Be a litter picker.

Sam Dibble (10)
Rector Drew School, Hawarden

Extinction

A ny animals can be extinct,
N ow animals are going to be extinct very soon.
I n our world we are lucky to have animals,
M any of us don't like our animals,
A nd that's why we should save our world,
L ike the panda, they are going soon.
S o what do you think?

Deryn Wakefield (11)
Rector Drew School, Hawarden

Endangered Species

Endangered species will become extinct easily,
If we hurt them or kill them.
If we do, they will become extinct easily.

Some endangered species are scared of humans,
So if they see a human and they run away
They will think you are going to hurt them.

Please stop hunting,
Hunting is bad,
It is bad for animals
Because they shouldn't get killed.

Leonie Thompson (8)
Richmond Hill Primary School, Aspatria

War

Homes are being destroyed
Because they are being bombed.
If you are not careful you might get bombed,
You will die.
So ban wars or you'll die!

Alix Long (8)
Richmond Hill Primary School, Aspatria

Talk!

War is a bad thing to do,
If you go to war you may die.

War is terrifying,
Right now a lot of destruction is going on.

So stop killing and sit down,
Talk, don't be violent.

Be smart,
Talk!

Jonathan Love (8)
Richmond Hill Primary School, Aspatria

Stopping War

Killing is very dangerous,
Someone can be seriously hurt,
War is a very dangerous thing,
Instead of bombing they should have a conversation.
When you are fighting you could die easily,
Their homes will get destroyed,
They will have nowhere to live.

Steven Crake (8)
Richmond Hill Primary School, Aspatria

War

I think instead of war
We should sit and talk,
To think of the violence and destruction
We have caused.
One day the world will be destroyed by war.
The way to stop this is to talk.

Matthew Charlton (8)
Richmond Hill Primary School, Aspatria

Deforestation

People have to leave their homes
Because people are cutting down trees.
People could die of no food and water
When people cut down trees,
They could kill people in lots of countries,
We won't have any oxygen.

Dylan McTear (8)
Richmond Hill Primary School, Aspatria

Knife Crime

Knife crime is very bad,
Robbers use knives to threaten,
They could stab you.
Police cars stop robbers.

Callum Rogers (8)
Richmond Hill Primary School, Aspatria

Rainforest/Destruction

R unning water going through the rainforest,
A waterfall is always in a rainforest.
I nsects crawling about everywhere in a rainforest.
N othing can beat the record of plants in a rainforest.
F ood is easy to find in a rainforest.
O xygen is everywhere in a rainforest.
R ipe fruits are found in a rainforest.
E verywhere, beauty is shone of green in a rainforest.
S torks are stalking in a rainforest.
T igers are growling fiercely in a rainforest.

D ying animals, because of pollution.
E verything destroyed in a second.
S ome parts of a rainforest are extinct.
T rucks pollute rainforests.
R ainforest trees are made into paper, but sometimes recycled.
U nder trees falling, homes are destroyed.
C ivilisation is getting destroyed.
T rees are falling and killing big animals as well.
I t is known that some rainforests are destroyed.
O ur rainforest tribes are dying.
N one of the trees are replanted when destroyed.

Srihari Prasad Bhallamudi (10)
Springfield Primary School, Tilehurst

Environment Poem

It is hard to look after the environment we live in,
We have to put litter in the bin,
Switch off the light when we go to bed,
Do not waste the wood when you put up sheds,
Never ever smoke on the streets,
Or waste electricity by using heat.
That's all I have to say,
So never waste CO_2 emissions ever again.

Anisa Kantharia
Tayyibah Girls' School, Stamford Hill

Child Labour!

The world can do itself a favour,
By preventing itself from child labour,
So listen to this carefully,
So children can play cheerfully.
Looking at children walking by,
We can't hear them when they sigh,
We can't see the child labour behind closed doors,
We can't see them doing many hard chores,
Working day in, day out,
Getting diseases from all about.
They work so hard that their knuckles start to bleed,
Some food and water is all they need,
They can't make their own choice,
They're innocent victims of your voice.
Making money is your delight,
But you don't care about their plight,
They are obeying all your commands,
And yet they don't have any demands.
Now that you know how they feel,
Soften that heart made of steel,
So go ahead, do a good action,
Donate some money to their satisfaction!

Suhaa Mahmood
Tayyibah Girls' School, Stamford Hill

You Should Care

We have to stop
And grow some crops,
Help the poor
To not have war,
Give them help
So they don't yelp.
Some people don't care
And are not fair,
Some people have wealth
And some don't have health.
I care, I really do,
So you should too,
No one likes death
And it's better to have breath.
Leave the families together,
So they sleep side by side forever,
Stop all bad
Because when I see them I feel sad.

Zaynab Almeriouh
Tayyibah Girls' School, Stamford Hill

Poor Children

Poor children with no home,
Just standing there all alone,
Walking all day on the streets,
Walking sadly, with bare feet.
Oh people, let's hold hands,
Together let's help them.
Always be generous,
Because children are penniless.
Now we've told you what to do,
It's time for you to help them too,
And don't forget that they will thank you.

Louisa Benatallah
Tayyibah Girls' School, Stamford Hill

Help The World

I write this poem very fast,
I write this poem so it can last,
I write this poem to save the world,
To especially help little boys and girls.
Endangered animals, those are so weak,
Endangered animals, those are so meek.
You've got to respect people who are poor,
You *have* to stop the war.
Help the animals in the sea,
Help them especially, just not for me.

I feel like crying, I feel so sad,
Stop the people who are so bad.
Help the people who don't have food,
Stop the people who are so rude.
So always remember to save the world,
And especially help little boys and girls.

Please, please help the world.

Nasimah Galiara
Tayyibah Girls' School, Stamford Hill

Bullies In My School

As I walk to school I see girls laughing and sniggering
Behind my back, which breaks my soul.
I wish I could tell them to be kind and not cruel.
I hate it when people bully,
I wish it could end fully.
Let the darkness of my life disappear,
While everyone is looking with one little stare.
My life is now ruined apart,
I can't come out of my house with a bully near
Because she might hurt me I fear.

Ayesha Chowdhury
Tayyibah Girls' School, Stamford Hill

Litter

Litter, litter tastes so bitter
In the bin should go your litter,
Recycle your tins and plastic
Into the bins.
Save the environment,
It's time to begin,
Everywhere you look,
Litter, litter,
Streets paved not with glitter
But litter.
If only you would use the bins,
Recycle your things.
Save the environment,
It's time to begin.
Litter, litter everywhere,
Litter, litter here and there.

Amina Atchoum
Tayyibah Girls' School, Stamford Hill

Help Me . . .

I don't want to be in child labour,
Working from dawn till dusk
From the age of 8 till grown up.
I don't want to sew, clean or be a match girl.
I work for nothing, just 10p a day,
Living off the streets,
No decent food for me to eat,
Nowhere cosy and warm to sleep.
The clothes I sew aren't for me,
But for children in a better place than me.
My life is hard; I wish I didn't live this life.
If only I had a family to care,
Then I wouldn't be in this despair.

Iman Atchoum
Tayyibah Girls' School, Stamford Hill

Sharada

My name is Sharada and I'm nine years old,
I don't have a mother or a father, neither a brother nor a sister.
My life is very hard, because I have to work,
I don't have any friends; I don't even go to school.
I'm a knitter. I knit jumpers, scarves, hats, etc.
I know you're thinking that India is a very hot place,
But know that there are floods, so it gets cold.
I think my pen is running out, but I'll carry on.
I'm quite hungry now, but my pay isn't due yet.
Oh, I wish I hadn't spent my money on a worthless pin wheel!
Well, it's getting quite dark now, so I think I'll have to go.
My last few words are: help a child like me,
Donate some money now.
Just 1p a day will help.
Thank you!

Tahani Ali
Tayyibah Girls' School, Stamford Hill

Child Labour

Children being hurt,
But still going to work.
Their parents have forgotten about them,
But there are still people feeling sorry for them.
You should let the children go to school,
They could pass their exams and when they grow up,
They'll choose a job they want to do.
You should see the children in the street,
Nobody wants them, nobody sees,
Some businessman who's really rich
Just picks them up, that makes me sick.
The way they torture the little kids.
If you give them a little money,
It would seem as if you made the whole world sunny.

Ilham Kemal
Tayyibah Girls' School, Stamford Hill

Bullying

Bullying is bad,
It makes other people sad,
I would have hated it if I got bullied,
Plus it isn't a very good deed.
I get upset if I see someone getting bullied,
I see that they're in a lot of need.
If someone tried to stop a bully
They will get beaten up fully.
I have not got bullied *yet,*
But once they caught me in a net.
Some bullies take other people's food,
They are also very rude.
Well, I really feel sorry for you if you get *bullied!*

Mariam Patel
Tayyibah Girls' School, Stamford Hill

Make The World A Better Place

Child labour, child labour, I care about you,
Child labour, child labour, and you should too.
Child labour - use your mind,
Child labour - there's many things you can find.

Litter, litter in the air,
Litter, litter everywhere.
Litter, litter, bring us more bins,
Litter, litter, like sharpened pins.

When you go out you can step on glass,
So take away the concrete, and instead grow grass.
Don't kill animals and so, instead, recycle things
To help make the world a better place!

Hadjar Sebaa
Tayyibah Girls' School, Stamford Hill

Bullying

Bullying is bad for you,
It can make you sad, it's true,
Don't hurt anyone's feelings,
So they don't end up stealing.
There are things in the world that you don't have to do,
But if you don't, things will happen to you.
Don't get sad,
And don't get mad,
Just tell the police.
But don't forget Mum and Dad!

Shakira Begum
Tayyibah Girls' School, Stamford Hill

Young Writers Information

We hope you have enjoyed reading this book - and that you will continue to enjoy it in the coming years.

If you like reading and writing poetry drop us a line, or give us a call, and we'll send you a free information pack.

Alternatively if you would like to order further copies of this book or any of our other titles, then please give us a call or log onto our website at www.youngwriters.co.uk

Young Writers Information
Remus House
Coltsfoot Drive
Peterborough
PE2 9JX
(01733) 890066